Edmund Blunden

Twayne's English Authors Series

Kinley E. Roby, Editor

Northeastern University

TEAS 344

EDMUND BLUNDEN
(1896–1974)
Photograph courtesy of Claire M. Blunden

Edmund Blunden

By Thomas Mallon

Vassar College

Twayne Publishers • Boston

Edmund Blunden

Thomas Mallon

Copyright © 1983 by G. K. Hall & Company
All Rights Reserved
Published by Twayne Publishers
A Division of G. K. Hall & Company
70 Lincoln Street
Boston, Massachusetts 02111

Book Production by Marne B. Sultz
Book Design by Barbara Anderson

Printed on permanent/durable acid-free
paper and bound in the United States of
America.

Library of Congress Cataloging in Publication Data

Mallon, Thomas, 1951—
   Edmund Blunden.

   (Twayne's English authors series; TEAS 344)
   Bibliography: p. 127
   Includes index.
   1. Blunden, Edmund, 1896—1974—Criticism and
interpretation. I. Title. II. Series.
PR6003.L8Z75   1983   821'.912   82—21370
ISBN   0—8057—6829—7

In memory of my father,
Arthur Vincent Mallon
1913–1980

". . . each day I keep my faith in you and life . . ."

Contents

About the Author

Thomas Mallon was born in 1951 and grew up in Stewart Manor, New York. He received the B.A. from Brown University and the M.A. and Ph.D. from Harvard, where he taught Expository Writing and English for several years. He has been Visiting Assistant Professor of English at Texas Tech University, and is now Assistant Professor at Vassar College. His articles and reviews have appeared in *Biography*, *Critique*, *Contemporary Literature*, *National Review*, and other journals, and he is currently working on a book about diaries.

Preface

More than sixty years have now passed since the First World War came to its exhausted end, and the phrase "World War I poetry" has, in the course of those years, come to represent a familiar body of writing to readers and scholars. The heroic early war sonnets of the gifted Rupert Brooke, the savage ironies of Siegfried Sassoon's *Counter-Attack* upon the glorious view of war, and the eloquent and funereal views of Wilfred Owen have gained a rightful and permanent place in our century's literature. Far less well known, however, are the war poems of Edmund Blunden, who wrote not only of his experiences as a very young soldier on the Western Front, but of the war's haunting of his imagination for decades after the Armistice of 1918. A surge of scholarly interest in the "war poets" during the last several years has produced fine new biographies of some of them, but despite the honor and attention he has received in such books as Paul Fussell's *The Great War and Modern Memory*, there remains no full-length study of Edmund Blunden's work.

During his long career, Blunden produced, in addition to his writings about the war, a large body of skillful and deeply felt poems concerning nature and life in the world of the English village. Those concerned with environmental causes today might be surprised to find among his works numerous poems and prose writings calling attention to the twentieth century's technological threats to the world of country men and country creatures. Blunden's close acquaintance with the natural world steered his philosophic turns of mind as well, and helped him in his fashioning of a deceptively casual body of poetry concerned with those metaphysical questions faced by every man in every time.

Blunden was also a gifted literary historian and biographer, and to his prolific production of poetry was added a formidable collection of critical works in prose on a wide variety of subjects. I first encountered Edmund Blunden when I was an undergraduate, through an essay of his on the early Tudor dramatist and poet John Skelton. It was, I later came to know, characteristic of his critical writings: celebratory, good-humored, more interested in exciting a reader about the text under discussion than in performing a scientific dismantling of it.

A full biography of Edmund Blunden remains to be written. My own book is designed to provide an overall critical introduction to Blunden's varied career and body of work. An initial chapter of biographical information is followed by chapters which examine his nature, village, war, and philosophic poetry. That examination is followed by a brief survey of his critical and biographical writings (which are alluded to frequently in discussion of the poetry), and the progress of Blunden's own critical reputation over the last half-century is surveyed. This approach, essentially thematic rather than chronological, has been adopted as the most useful one, because Blunden's work is less remarkable for changes in subject and style than for its continued exploration of several realms of human and literary experience which held his attention and devotion for a lifetime.

A certain amount of advocacy accompanies analysis in most places. This is not done in any earnest attempt to tamper with conventional literary rankings, but simply to make the case that Blunden's work has not reached as many readers as it should; if his place in the development of twentieth-century literature will probably never be considered very large, it should be more easily discoverable than it is. An effort is also made in these pages to see Blunden as a successor to some earlier English poetic strains, particularly those "undertones" he knew so well.

In the course of my research I was fortunate to have been able to draw not only upon published material by and about Blunden, but upon the large quantity of manuscripts, correspondence, and diaries now housed in American libraries. I owe a debt to the staffs of the Houghton Library of Harvard University, the Berg Collection of the New York Public Library, and the Humanities Research Center of the University of Texas at Austin—especially Mrs. Ellen Dunlap and Mr. David Farmer—for providing access to and permission to quote various materials. I am extremely indebted to Mrs. Edmund Blunden, not only for the delight of her conversation and hospitality during my trips to Suffolk and Cambridge, but also for providing great quantitites of information and encouragement. I would like to thank Sir Rupert Hart-Davis, the late Mr. Robert Lowell, and Professor Paul Engle of the University of Iowa for answering my inquiries and providing me with information and materials. Sheila McIlwraith of the A. D. Peters literary agency in London and Kenkyusha Publishers in Tokyo also provided me with assistance, and I am grateful. Professor Chau Wah Ching, a former student of Edmund Blunden's in Hong Kong, was kind enough to read part of the manuscript. I hope that many others will realize that my gratitude is warmer than the rather formal "Acknowledgments" given them may indicate.

Preface

The kindness and insights of many people at Harvard University were important to me in the preparation of this book. Chief among these was Professor Robert Kiely, who was always generous with his time and advice—even when he was an ocean away, spending a sabbatical in Rupert Brooke's "Old Vicarage" in Grantchester. I am also grateful to many friends and colleagues at Vassar College for their practical assistance and sensible advice.

Thomas Mallon

Vassar College

Acknowledgments

Grateful acknowledgment is made to the following for permission to quote from the materials indicated:

The Edmund Blunden Estate and A. D. Peters & Co. Ltd., for poems, prose, letters, and manuscripts of Edmund Blunden.

The Humanities Research Center, The University of Texas at Austin, for manuscript materials by and relating to Edmund Blunden.

The Henry W. and Albert A. Berg Collection, The New York Public Library, Astor, Lenox and Tilden Foundations, for letters written by and concerning Edmund Blunden.

The Houghton Library of Harvard University for Edmund Blunden's letter to Robert Lowell.

Sir John Betjeman for his letter to Edmund Blunden.

Mr. Frank Bidart and the Estate of the late Mr. Robert Lowell for Mr. Lowell's letter to Edmund Blunden.

The Estate of the late Richard Church for his letters to Edmund Blunden.

Mrs. Jill Day Lewis for C. Day Lewis's letter to Edmund Blunden and "Lines for Edmund Blunden on his Fiftieth Birthday."

The Trustees of the estate of the late Miss E. A. Dugdale for Florence Hardy's letter to Edmund Blunden.

Professor Paul Engle for a letter written to him by Edmund Blunden.

Miss Jennifer Gosse for letters from Sir Edmund Gosse to Edmund Blunden.

Mr. Robert Graves for his letter to Edmund Blunden and extracts from *Good-bye to All That.*

Mr. J. Robert Haines for Ivor Gurney's letter to Edmund Blunden.

Sir Rupert Hart-Davis, for letters from Siegfried Sassoon to Edmund Blunden, and for his own funeral address for Edmund Blunden.

David Higham Associates Ltd., for Edward Marsh's letter to Edmund Blunden.

Professor John Jones for letters of H. W. Garrod to Edmund Blunden.

Mr. Frank Magro and the estate of the late Sir Osbert Sitwell for Sir Osbert's letter to Edmund Blunden.

Dr. D. A. Parry, for E. M. Forster's letter to Edmund Blunden, ©The Provost and Scholars of King's College, Cambridge.

Chronology

1896 Edmund Blunden born 1 November in London.

1900 The Blundens move to Yalding, Kent.

1907 Blunden enters Cleave's Grammar School.

1909 Enters Christ's Hospital.

1914 Becomes "Senior Grecian" at the school.

1915 Leaves Christ's Hospital. Joins 11th Royal Sussex Regiment.

1916 Service in France begins. Awarded the Military Cross.

1918 Marries Mary Daines.

1919 Returns from France. Briefly takes up a scholarship at Queen's College, Oxford. Receives financial assistance from Edward Marsh and begins serious career as a poet. Death of his infant daughter, Joy.

1920 Lives on Boar's Hill, near Oxford, home of other poets such as Robert Graves. Moves to London and becomes J. Middleton Murry's assistant on the *Athenaeum*. *The Waggoner* and *John Clare: Poems Chiefly from Manuscript*, edited with Alan Porter, are published.

1922 Takes sea voyage to South America to aid recovery from lingering physical and nervous effects of the war. *The Shepherd* awarded the Hawthornden Prize for poetry. *The Bonadventure*, account of his South American voyage, is published.

1923 *Christ's Hospital: A Retrospect.*

1924 Becomes Professor of English Literature, Tokyo University.

1925 *English Poems.*

1927 Returns to England from Japan. *On the Poems of Henry Vaughan* is published.

1928 Resumes work for the *Nation*. *Undertones of War, Retreat*, and *Leigh Hunt's "Examiner" Examined* are published.

1929 *Nature in English Literature* published by Hogarth Press. *Near and Far: New Poems.*

1930 Lives at Hawstead Place near Bury St. Edmunds with his brother

Gilbert and sister-in-law Annie. Gathers material for *The Face of England*. *Poems 1914–30*, his first comprehensive collection, and *Leigh Hunt*, his first full literary biography, are published.

1931   Becomes Fellow and Tutor in English Literature, Merton College, Oxford. *Votive Tablets*, a collection of critical essays, and his edition of *Poems of Wilfred Owen* are published. Divorced from Mary Daines.

1932   Gives Clark Lectures on Charles Lamb at Cambridge University.

1933   Marries Sylva Norman, the novelist and critic. *We'll Shift Our Ground*, written with her, and *Charles Lamb and His Contemporaries*, the previous year's Clark Lectures.

1934   *Choice or Chance* and *The Mind's Eye*, a collection of essays on war, literature, Japan, and rural England.

1936   *Keats's Publisher: A Memoir of John Taylor*.

1937   *An Elegy and Other Poems*.

1940   Begins service as Staff Member, Oxford Senior Training Corps. *Poems 1930–40*.

1941   *English Villages*.

1942   *Thomas Hardy*. Writes introduction for *Poems of this War*. Divorced from Sylva Norman.

1944   *Cricket Country* and *Shells by a Stream*.

1945   Marries Claire Margaret Poynting. Four daughters are born to them in the next decade.

1946   *Shelley: A Life Story*.

1947   Returns to Japan, after two decades, with United Kingdom Liaison Mission; during next three years gives hundreds of lectures on English literature and culture.

1949   *Sons of Light: A Series of Lectures on English Writers* and *After the Bombing*.

1950   Elected to the Japan Academy (honorary). *Chaucer to "B. V."* and *A Wanderer in Japan* are published. Returns to England to write for *Times Literary Supplement*.

1951   Made a Commander of the Order of the British Empire.

1953   Becomes Professor of English Literature at the University of Hong Kong; teaches there with Mrs. Blunden for the next decade.

1956   Awarded Queen's Gold Medal for Poetry.

1957   *Poems of Many Years*, his most comprehensive collection, is published.

1959   *Three Young Poets: Critical Sketches of Byron, Shelley and Keats.*

1961   *Edmund Blunden: Sixty-Five*, a book of tributes from writers, colleagues, students and friends is published and presented to him on his birthday.

1962   *A Hong Kong House.*

1963   Inducted into Order of the Rising Sun, Third Class, in Japan.

1964   Returns to England and retires to Hall Mill, Long Melford, Suffolk.

1965   *Eleven Poems*, his final collection, is published.

1966   Elected Professor of Poetry at Oxford over the American poet Robert Lowell amidst considerable publicity.

1968   Poor health forces his resignation.

1970   Awarded Midsummer Prize, Corporation of London.

1974   Dies at Hall Mill, Long Melford, on 20 January.

Chapter One
The Writer Himself:
A Brief Biography

The Man of the Country

With his death in Suffolk on 20 January 1974, Edmund Blunden passed into the literary history he had examined so lovingly in his prose, and whose traditions he had sustained in over a half-century of writing poetry. He became a subject. He well knew that as his presence receded the biographical impulse would reach out to it. He would not object; he understood that impulse, and had himself executed its demands with skill and elegance. It had even been the subject of some of his poems. He once described Thornton Hunt's editing of his father's, Leigh Hunt's, correspondence; at first it seemed a matter of "Dead Letters," but

> more and more these nameless annals clutched
> The hasty hand, the heart, till a hundred ghosts
> Of men unlauded, past and gone,
> Seemed friends that we had always known. [1]

As he reminded a Japanese audience, Samuel Johnson "knew perfectly well" a truth of biography that remains in force: "most of us are more likely to make friends with a writer's works if we know something about the writer himself." [2] So it is fitting to begin a discussion of Blunden's own writing with some talk about his life; and since Blunden's own personality was an appealing one, this biographical task has its own rewards beyond interpretive ones.

It no doubt surprises some readers of English pastoral poetry to find out that on 1 November 1896, Edmund Blunden was born not in a village in Kent or Sussex, but at 54a Tottenham Court Road in London. [3] Charles Edmund Blunden and Georgina Tyler had been married the year before. When Edmund Charles was born "they were sharing the headship of a school in London, but as the family increased so did their desire to return to the country; they happened on the quiet Kentish village of

Yalding. . . ."[4] It was here that Edmund spent his early years. The future poet was actually returning to the rural world of his ancestors. His grandfather and namesake, who died shortly after Edmund's birth, had been a farm bailiff in Maidstone; a letter he wrote to his son, the poet's father, about his marriage to Georgina is revealing in its sympathy, honesty, good humor, and attention to the details of country life and country language. These were all to be the loves and poetic preoccupations of his grandson, and they are all present in the letter written from Asylum Farm on 17 December 1895:

Dear Charlie

Rec^d. yours this afternoon glad to hear your Mother arrived safely you had better give her plenty of room

M^r. Leney has been here since I commenced this scrible he had some Stout & drank to your health & happiness.

Saw M^r. Buss early in the afternoon he is sending some fruit off this evening to be delivered & will send some Flowers to morrow evening so you can send to Holborn Station as early as you like on Thursday morning.

M^r. John Brown brought a pair of Salt^s made of polished wood with metal hoops, resembles a Beer barrel cut in halves, with the usual wishes, shall not send them up you can take them with you when you go up after the holidays

M^r. Duncan Smith. is going to give you a Coal (something). I quite forget what he called it but in Plain English it would be called a scuttle.

I think that is all I have got to write about at present except to be kindly remembered to all concerned
                    I remain with best wishes for your welfare,
                                        E. Blunden

P. S. Dont forget to get two Bears to keep in your house, *Bear and Forbear*, (advice for both)[5]

The poet's parents taught in Yalding from 1900 to 1912. Charles Blunden "was also organist and choirmaster, and had much to do with village concerts. . . . As head master at Yalding [he] was generally admired for sensible teaching and discipline; he related his work to the life of the agricultural community, in those days still compact and contented. In early autumn he was often employed as manager in the hopgardens, which brought him odd friends from the East End of London; but he had the art of winning both liking and respect anywhere."[6] The deterioration of the "agricultural community" hinted at in this passage from an unpublished memoir, as well as the hop-picking referred to, would recur frequently as theme and motif in Edmund Blunden's writings. Far less conspicuous would be the family hardships which were endured. Charles Blunden "was awkwardly placed between the class in the big houses and the farm labourers and small tradesmen. The division was then quite rigid,"[7] and this positioning made for economic woes as well as injuries to his sensitivity. Nine children were born to the Blundens between 1896 and 1909, "and the difficulty of keeping the home going led to money troubles. As the schoolhouse was rather small, the family moved to Old Congelow, a farmhouse, fabled to have a ghost. Other removals followed, and at last we occupied a cottage opposite The Anchor Inn at Twyford."[8] In 1908 Charles suffered a kind of breakdown over these troubles.[9] Years later, Blunden recalled him as a figure who inevitably reminds one of John Dickens, father of the great novelist: "he painted bright migrations & brighter destinations, & his children ridiculed him; with that the sense of being much discussed & dissected hurt him. . . . In Yalding he had spent 12 years, and he left it while still in debt & now and then in despair. . . . He did not content himself with borrowing money: he lent it with much greater ease, & gave at the door & at the bar beyond all reason."[10] It is one of the minor ironies of the history of literature and debt that one of the items "sold up" from the Blunden house to pay creditors was a complete set of the works of Charles Dickens.

In 1913 the Blundens were appointed to the Framfield School in Sussex (where they had served briefly in 1899 between London and Yalding); during the First World War, Charles did supply work and served as schoolmaster on the training ship *Mount Edgecumbe*, at Saltash. From 1919 until his retirement in 1930 he served a final headmastership at Salcombe, South Devon. Then he retired to Yalding, where he lived past his eighty-first birthday in 1952. Overcoming earlier difficulties, he gradually came to be known "as a representative of an age of wisdom and security. He bore himself upright as he walked, carefully dressed in an old-fashioned way without any attempt to be archaic, to a great age. The second World War, when bombs fell near his house, seemed only to confirm him in the view that humanity is still imperfectly educated and will remain so, if anything remains."[11]

Blunden's private memoir is tender in its recitation of his father's troubles and his own childish reactions to them. But Charles Blunden also had his share of untroubled hours and talents, and it is these that his son put into the published poems and prose writings centered on his father. Charles Blunden the cricketer, angler, kind and competent schoolmaster and churchman—this is the essential figure in the pre-1914 village landscape that Edmund Blunden was to celebrate as his ideal for half a century. The shadows surrounding his father are

scattered for the sake of the larger vision. In the elegy "An Empty
Chair (Chas. E. B.)," Blunden remembered him as a man "loving those
earth-skills (thought little of) / By which the whole's sustained."[12]
And whatever difficulties there were in his own youthful world, there
were still the cricket grounds, the streams and rivers (especially the
Teise), and books in the house to work happily on Edmund Blunden's
natural imagination. He recalled this world in *The Face of England*:
"I can fairly say, not forgetting those miseries which childhood only
understands as miseries, that life was not so bad in that Kentish village
before the war. London was within forty miles of us, but troubled most
of the inhabitants hardly more than the mountains of the moon."[13]

Blunden attended Cleave's Grammar School in Yalding before going
to Christ's Hospital in Horsham. This latter school, which when located
in London had produced such "Old Blues" as Coleridge, Leigh Hunt,
and Charles Lamb, deeply affected his literary and historic imagination;
he would later write its history and contribute to the scholarship of many
of its eminent graduates. Blunden's early career there, before he was
"Senior Grecian" in 1914, was recalled decades later by A. C. W.
Edwards, housemaster: "Apparently here was the really perfect boy,
keen as mustard in class and in games, who was eccentric in one respect
only—he wrote poems. Good ones too. I made haste to get to know him.
I found him a nervous-speaking, weakly-built boy, bulging with brains
and bursting with enthusiasms."[14] The "Beaky Bard" was also a bare-
handed cricketer who rose to be Captain of the School.[15] Here, "[w]here
Lamb once passed, the master soul," Blunden's early awareness of the
traditions of the English countryside had added to it an almost palpable
sense of literary history.

Some small collections of poems, some of which he had written for the
school magazine, the *Blue*, were soon printed at Uckfield and Horsham,
where Shelley's first poems had gone to press with money provided by his
grandfather. In the more substantial collection of *Pastorals* printed in
London in 1916, Blunden, in "The Preamble," called upon the reader to
"[l]isten, and learn the delights that have passioned the heart of a boy."
His inspiration and purpose were simple:

> I sing of the rivers and hamlets and woodlands
>   of Sussex and Kent,
> Such as I know them. . . .[16]

He seemed at Christ's Hospital to be on a precocious way toward
becoming a prolific, skillful and largely untroubled—except in a some-

times conventionally gloomy adolescent way—poet of the countryside. In 1914 he won the Senior Classics scholarship to Queen's College, Oxford. All was quick progress.

The Everlasting Front

But the Great War arrived to split his life and consciousness in two. It had been not too threateningly on the horizon during the last spring at Christ's Hospital, and even during a visit to Oxford, after August 1914, it did not seem as if it would turn Western Europe into the charnel house that was soon to be constructed. In late 1914, Blunden remembered: "Soldiers from our village 'doing their bit' 'over in France today' wrote normal-sounding letters which got round. Many for all their gallant enlistment were still somewhere not in France at all. The battalion which I was eventually to join was not sent over there until the spring of 1916."[17] But that was the year of the battle of the Somme, which changed poetry and war, and perhaps even history, although not in the way intended. By that time the men in their columns were moving "fast as corks on a millstream, without complaint into the bondservice of destruction."[18] The day Blunden was to leave for the battlefield, he wrote in a darker version of Wordsworth's image of sailing from boyhood into the future, "drew as suddenly near / As drifting boats are tugged at last down to the glutting weir."[19] He went with the Royal Sussex Regiment to France and Belgium; commissioned in 1915, he was awarded the Military Cross one year later. He was gassed, and his lungs were to be troublesome until his death. He survived two years of combat, and when the Armistice was signed in November 1918 he was little more than a week past his twenty-second birthday.

Now the schoolboy pastoralist was one of the "war poets." His own contribution to the literature of that tragedy was to be his particular and tortured way of *recollecting* it. He was never able or willing to put a final stamp on his ghostly and shifting memories. He was one of the last prominent war poets left alive, and the war was one of the most living components of his imagination to the end. He also remained devoted to the work of the other war poets, assiduously tending their reputations when they could no longer do so themselves. The war was the kiln of his imagination. Before 1914 that faculty had already been growing, naturally and comfortably, into one that was "conservative" in most political and literary respects. But now the village home, recalled as it was before the war, became a kind of Eden. Blunden, in his seventies, admitted that there was a certain naiveté in his idealization: "my outlook was limited because my young days were spent almost wholly in pleasant places in the south of England. I was once in later years severely reprimanded by the poet Ralph Hodgson for having any opinions whatever on England in 1914 when I had never been so far north as Nottingham."[20] Still, the ghastliness of the war provided the antithesis necessary to transform what had been merely pleasant reality into the Arcadian vision that was to dominate much of his work.

The Young Poet-Critic

Immediately after the war he began his serious work as a poet. He wrote mostly as a survivor and custodian, and this conservancy was sometimes misread as complacency. More often it was actually closer to a kind of desperation. As he wrote more than a decade after his discharge, a harvest was for him an exciting occasion, "for, after the series of sudden chasms which my life has been, I am apt to regard some things as though they might never be vouchsafed to me in their intimacy again."[21]

This is the impulse that drove Blunden deeper and deeper into the country world—a more intense and complicated impulse than the one that drove most of the Georgian poets of the day there. Even so, Blunden's name has been continually linked with theirs, largely because of his appearance in *Georgian Poetry V*, the last of the widely selling anthologies edited by Edward Marsh, in 1922. Earlier, Marsh had had "a little fund to dispose of arising from the profits of [his] memoir of Rupert Brooke,"[22] and Blunden had shyly accepted what was "an absolute godsend. My handwriting shows it—I can very seldom write except when not harried nor anxious. I thank you with all my heart 'for this Relief.'"[23] In some ways Blunden was to Marsh what John Clare, the nineteenth-century peasant poet who was Blunden's most enduring literary enthusiasm, had been to John Taylor, his publisher: "a problem which . . . was distinctly congenial to him. Not himself a creative writer, he had a critical intelligence which sought to employ itself in the service of the imagination."[24] This was Marsh's relationship to many young poets, but his letters to Blunden are particularly fond and protective: the two men corresponded frequently over the next decade.

Still, for all Marsh's assistance, Blunden has suffered over the years from his link to the Georgians; less discerning critics have carelessly included him in their indictment of Georgian poetry for its general bloodlessness. Marsh, however, was not the only man who helped Blunden get started. The editors H. M. Tomlinson and J. C. Squire, and the recently famous Siegfried Sassoon—to whom he remained close for most of the next half-century—also acclimatized Blunden to the world of the periodical, and for both better and worse his work has been grouped with theirs.

After leaving the army, Blunden briefly took up his scholarship at Oxford, but that sum was not designed to support both himself and Mary Daines, the young woman he married in 1918. That marriage was to end unhappily, but it produced three children: Joy, who died in infancy and was to become the subject of a number of elegies over the next decades, and then John and Clare, named for Blunden's poetic idol and first critical subject. Blunden was, in any event, reaching an early poetic maturity, and he wanted to devote most of his energy to that rather than to finishing a degree. He settled briefly on Boar's Hill, the home of several other poets, including Robert Graves and Robert Bridges. With ample opportunities for critical reaction from his fellow poets, and a country woman for a wife, who supplied him with lore and solid country works, Blunden produced his early major work.[25]

This period at Oxford and Boar's Hill was also the one in which Blunden began his literary scholarship. With the aid of Alan Porter, who later taught at Vassar College, and Mary, he discovered a wealth of John Clare manuscripts at Peterborough and Northampton and published his own edition of them.[26] This was to be the first of many projects devoted to the resurrection of largely forgotten and troubled figures in English literary history. Blunden no doubt identified with Clare in this time of problems and poetic testing; as he wrote in his biography of Hardy years later, "the fate of a John Clare or a Jude Fawley is still within the bounds of possibility, under different externals."[27] But Blunden managed to escape their hard outcomes, and his work on Clare became most important as the beginning of his exercise of a gentle, celebrating critical attitude. The voice in his criticism quickly became as recognizable as the one in his poetry. He came to English literature "with the utmost reverence and sense of responsibility; I would go softly, and receive or give short instructions cautiously."[28]

In 1920 he went to London, the better to earn a living in the day-to-day literary world. During the early part of the new decade he was J. Middleton Murry's assistant on the *Athenaeum* and traveled on the edges of the circles which revolved around Murry and his wife, Katherine Mansfield, Philip and Ottoline Morrell, and Leonard and Virginia Woolf. *The Waggoner* (1920) and *The Shepherd* (1922) were warmly received and helped to set him apart, at least somewhat, from the "Squirearchy" of "Neo-Georgian" poets whose names were associated with J. C. Squire.

But success was neither easy nor uninterrupted. The war was still very much with him in its physical and emotional aftereffects, and near the beginning of 1922 his editors at the *Athenaeum* dispatched him on a voyage to South America aboard a cargo steamer by way of a healthful change. One of those editors was H. M. Tomlinson, who wrote that "in spite of his indispensability to his journal, we could not pretend any longer that Blunden's smile was not becoming discarnate, like that of the Cheshire Cat. So he was cleared out, while there was some of him to save . . . Blunden thinks we were kind to him; the truth is, we could not bear him on the conscience a day longer."[29] The result was Blunden's travel book *The Bonadventure*, which Mrs. Thomas Hardy, who with her husband in the early 1920s entertained Blunden and Siegfried Sassoon at Max Gate, reported that Mr. Hardy liked "exceedingly, though of course he much prefers your poems &, I think, rather grudges your writing a line of prose."[30]

Difficulties both financial and emotional continued; by 1924 the Blundens' marriage had been strained for a long period.[31] An opportunity arose that year for Blunden to take over the professorship of English literature that Robert Nichols had held at Tokyo Imperial University, and he accepted, thereby continuing the line of American and English writers in Japan begun by Lafcadio Hearn in the late nineteenth century. His English colleagues there between 1924 and 1927 included the writers Ralph Hodgson, Sherard Vines, and William Plomer. The Japanese scholar Takeshi Saito was instrumental in bringing Blunden so far from his poetry's subject and inspiration; it was Saito's attractive personality which helped cause Hodgson to take such a surprising step as well. What Blunden wrote of Hodgson's decision applies equally well to his own: "Such a move would never have been expected by those who knew the poet; he appeared to be inseparable from life in England, of which he was a tireless and romantic student."[32] But even as a child Blunden had had a fascination for Japan, recorded in the poem "Looking Eastward,"[33] and remembrance of it helped him to take the bold step of signing a contract on 12 March 1924 that provided him with 3,600 yen in traveling expenses, 660 yen per month, part of his house rent, and the assurance that he would not have to teach on Sundays.[34]

After a difficult start he became a revered teacher and presence, the trainer of a generation of Japanese scholars of English literature. In contrast to the somewhat regal Nichols, Blunden took lodgings that were modest, and "without the slightest ceremony, students would go to [his] hotel, singly or in groups, and talk for hours with [him] about

English poetry and literature."[35] He helped found the English Reading Society and carefully considered the poetry written by his own students. His shy and generous personality never found a more suitable home, and the number and quality of tributes to him from the Japanese, which have never ceased, are remarkable.

The Japan years, although ones of devoted service to literature and young people, were often personally troubling. Blunden's poems for new and substantial collections continued to mount up, but he suffered from homesickness, occasionally just typical, but at other times genuinely debilitating. And although the Japanese experience may have refined and deepened his poetry somewhat, there was no radical change in either vision or method. Blunden himself worried over the seeming intractability of his imagination:

> I have been wandering distant roads, have striven
> To win new comprehensions; much in vain.
> There's that within me cares not what is given
> By such migrations . . . .[36]

In his letters to Edward Marsh, Blunden wrote amusingly of the routine and humorous frustrations of exile, but the most painful difficulties of this period were absence from home at a time when his marriage was uncertain, separation from his two children, and, perhaps above all, the persistence of his war memories. During the Tokyo winter, the "wind blew sharper, and in [his] dreams [he] was frequently reporting for duty among wild shapes of war in snow-strewn morasses."[37] But the lengthened distances of geography and time between himself and the war, and the absence of such raw materials as his own copybooks and diaries, freed him to write about it in the particular retrospective way for which he was best suited. In Japan he was at last able to deal with war's "undertones"—and it was in Tokyo that he produced the quiet prose memoir that was to establish his reputation among a wider audience than ever before.

The bond he established with the Japanese was strong, and he would return to Asia for a long period two decades later, but 1927 seemed like the time to return to the real center of his emotional life and the source of his poetry. He went back to England to work, through 1930, on the amalgamated *Nation and Athenaeum* under Leonard Woolf. He was once again living the literary journalist's life with the vengeance of necessity: "he had, by his own generosity, made himself responsible for the upkeep of some six or seven other people, young and old. This meant that journalism and lecturing occupied most of his time, with poetry fitted into the cracks. His industry, then and always, was immense, as he meticulously wrote millions of words and countless letters in his beautiful handwriting."[38] The year 1930 saw the collected publication of poems written since 1914, and the printing of *Leigh Hunt*, his first full-length literary biography, on which he had been at work intermittently for the last decade. In this period he became a Fellow of the Royal Society of Literature.[39] In 1931 his literary essays were collected as *Votive Tablets*.

The Academic Life and War Once More

During 1930 Blunden lived with his brother Gilbert and sister-in-law Annie at Hawstead Place near Bury St. Edmunds in Suffolk. There he made the close observations of village life which he was to publish in *The Face of England* (1932), and prepared, as he approached his thirty-fourth birthday, for major changes in his own life. He was divorced from Mary, and he made ready to begin an academic career, which he hoped would prove more conducive to financial security and the writing of poetry than incessant journalism was proving. In 1931 he was elected to Merton College; he served as a Fellow and a Tutor for the next decade. In 1932 he gave the Clark Lectures at Cambridge, taking Charles Lamb, another Old Blue, as his subject. In 1933 he married Sylva Norman, the novelist and literary critic; that year the two of them published a collaborative novel, *We'll Shift Our Ground; or, Two on a Tour*, based on their experiences traveling to the old battlefields of the First World War—locations Blunden was to visit frequently, almost compulsively, for many years to come, for both personal reasons and for his work with the War Graves Commission. In a poem written to mark his thirty-fifth birthday on 1 November 1931, he uneasily accepted what he knew was to be his lifetime "knack / Of being always on the bivouac. . . ."[40]

The testimony of fellow Mertonians such as H. W. Garrod attests to Blunden's excellence as a teacher. Earl Miner has written that "many people feel the modern distinction of Merton College in English literature dates from the years he was a tutor. His presence and personality were integral parts of the revival."[41] His students included the critic Northrop Frye, the American poet Paul Engle, and a British poet of the next war, Keith Douglas.

There were three new volumes of poems in the 1930s, which were in turn selected from for a larger collection published in 1940. A collection of essays on various subjects appeared as *The Mind's Eye* in 1934, and the biography of John Taylor, *Keats's Publisher*, was published in 1936. There was also, as it turned out, for reasons of finance and devotion, a continuation of literary journalism, scholarly contributions, and work for the Book Society. As he wrote Sylva Norman in 1933, he was working under "this perpetual compulsion to invent something to say. . . ."[42]

The pressures of production were overshadowed, however, by the approach of the Second World War. The growing inevitability of another convulsion in Europe caused him tremendous pain, although he met it with all the good cheer he could summon. He had to watch a new generation of young men be pulled from England to the battlefield. Shortly after the invasion of Poland in 1939, on a day his asthma—a reminder of the First War—was troubling him, he recorded in his diary how illness and gloom were keeping him from his self-appointed task of doing justice in his writings "to the neglected multitude of poets and prose men who had made their mark once." But he shook this mood from himself, challenging "even this war as a final blow."[43]

When the war came, Blunden served as an instructor in the Oxford Senior Training Corps, but he left his other teaching to return to London and nearly full-time journalism for the *Times Literary Supplement*. Practical matters again forced this, a well as a general and defiant desire for a new beginning in the face of war. His two surviving children by Mary, now grown, had been raised apart from him, and he wanted to begin a family of his own. His marriage to Sylva Norman had not given him that, and at Oxford he had fallen in love with the much younger Claire Poynting. They were able to marry in 1945.

The war years, despite all private difficulties, turned out to be customarily productive. His biography of Hardy, researched at Merton in the early days of the war, appeared in 1942; his study of Shelley came in 1946. His ancient interests in husbandry and cricket also sustained him. The first led to participation in the promotion of an agrarian political and economic philosophy being put forward by, among others, H. J. Massingham. The second resulted in *Cricket Country* (1944), a book chiefly about his much-loved sport, but one which allowed him to expound upon a number of philosophical and conservation concerns as well. The preservation of rural England had become an increasingly prominent theme in his poetry and prose in the last decade. The war years also allowed him to participate more fully in literary society. Laurence Brander has recalled a number of encounters with Blunden in this period, "for example, a lively discussion on a Shakespeare play in a London cellar between Blunden and Forster and Orwell. . . . He was working on *The Times Literary Supplement* then and I was in Amen House not far away. We would meet and eat sandwiches and hurry down the Farringdon Road, in a sort of goldrush spirit. What treasures would the book barrows have that day?"[44]

Elder Literary Statesman

Shells by a Stream appeared in 1944. The war ended, and, newly and happily married, the Blundens began a family that was eventually to include four daughters. Despite the atomic world's ever-increasing capacity for war and terror, to which he would continue to respond in his poetry, the early postwar years began a period of stability such as Blunden had not known since the days before August 1914. After two more years with the *TLS*, he returned to Japan as a kind of literary statesman, when he was appointed to the United Kingdom Liaison Mission in Tokyo in 1947.

In less than three years Blunden "gave about 600 lectures in Tokyo and other larger cities all over this war-devastated country . . . , performing prodigious work with almost superhuman energy far in excess of what his duty laid upon him."[45] Many of those lectures have been collected and published in Japan, and they form a worthy part of Blunden's enormous critical output. Precisely because they were usually put on a "simple" level to accommodate an audience of nonnative speakers of English, they are a remarkable exercise in criticism; they cut, of necessity, to the essentials of a writer, genre, or period. Devoid of any academic fuss, they do much to illuminate Blunden's passions in English literature. They also helped to sustain the growing tradition of English literary study in Japan whose beginnings Blunden had nurtured a generation before. In 1950 he was elected an honorary member of the Japan Academy—the same year Albert Einstein was inducted.[46] In 1963, on one of several return visits, he was awarded the Order of the Rising Sun, Third Class. His influence in Japan continues to the present day.

There were also honors in his own country; he was made a Commander, Order of the British Empire and a C. Lit. by the Royal Society of Literature, and he received the Queen's Gold Medal for Poetry in 1956. But these recognitions did not carry remunerative attachments sufficient to support his growing family. Blunden had returned to England in 1950 to go back to work at the *TLS*, but that could not be a permanent solution. The pressures of journalism again proved too great. As he wrote Leonard Clark in June 1953: "Life is a sheer stampede, and I am really a tired old hawk."[47]

A steadier future lay in Asia, and in 1953 he accepted the offer of a professorship of English literature at the University of Hong Kong. He remained for more than a decade, Mrs. Blunden teaching with him in the English department, leaving behind a reputation almost as substantial as the one he made in Japan. University life made its own great demands on his time, however, and his "output" in the 1950s was not as large as it had been in the past; but poems continued to be written. There was another collected edition in 1957, and a final major collection in 1962, *A Hong Kong House*. Blunden was again away from his main poetic wellspring, the countryside of England, but his pastoral vision continued to hold him, and it was renewed by the challenges he threw out to the growing technological threat with the vigor of their "fresh Common Nouns,"[48] hardier survivals than many of the poems of his "fellow" Georgians.

In 1964 Blunden retired to England, purchasing his home, Hall Mill in Long Melford, Sudbury, Suffolk, with the aid of his old friend Sassoon.[49] A last collecton of *Eleven Poems* appeared in 1965. His most public, and controversial (see Chapter 6), recognition came in 1966, as he neared seventy, when he was elected Professor of Poetry at Oxford, the chair that Matthew Arnold had once held. Ill health forced him before long to discontinue the occasional lectures that were the chief duty of the post.

The "long twilight of his last years" had begun.[50] His young daughters and wife gave him a lively present, but more and more he was aware that he was the last survivor of a long war and pilgrimage. As the end of his life approached he would think increasingly of the cataclysm that marked the beginning of its maturity. Late in 1967 he wrote Leonard Clark:

I don't go about much, or would ask your hospitality more often. I feel my age, especially since Siegfried's departure. [Sassoon had died that year.] Our girls dominate the scene, except that Fan is not on it, being some sort of help in a household in Paris. We may yet find her charging in for Christmas. I was strangely exculpated from War I one day in Flanders, but a certain infinity has [chased?] me back there and I want to find the way out, which will be duly shown.[51]

He died in Long Melford on 20 January 1974, his last major work—a biography of Coleridge, another Blue—unfinished.[52]

The Force of Personality

"He has goodness; he has wisdom."[53] This is how Laurence Brander simply put his description of Blunden's personality. One is struck again and again by the gentleness of that personality, its sweetness and goodness reflected not only in the words of friends, but in the works themselves. For all the horror he had seen, he maintained a quietly heroic faith and perseverance. In *A Hong Kong House* he recorded his feelings and wishes "On Tearing Up a Cynical Poem":

> Justice and Mercy and Childhood, gods, move still
> Among us; all our utterances direct,
> Governing our biasses. The heavenly hill
> Undarken from our scornful intellect.
> Shine, Powers, and light the world with lily-truth,
> Preventing death armed with the cynic tooth.[54]

This good will has sometimes been mistaken for an easy contentment by commentators, and there has been a tendency to look at Blunden's poetry as all of a piece. What has been lost is the truth that he was a poet of many themes; indeed, Blunden is perhaps best reached through an examination of ideas. His own Hardyesque note of caution, that he made no "attempt to deliver an elaborated philosophy through the separate productions (in many instances) of varying impulse and circumstance," is to be remembered.[55] Nevertheless, there is real usefulness in attempting to isolate his poems on the natural world, the world of the village, war and its aftereffects, and metaphysical questions, one group from the others, even as one attempts to create a picture of his entire imagination. Within his themes, there is a certain consistency—"The Home of Poetry" was located in the earliest days and places of his life. After his travels he realizes: "The narrow fence / Of first things is song's liberty. Returning, / I hail magnificence."[56] Experience changed his mind and art more than is admitted here, of course; the war was especially profound proof of this. Still, we do recognize the poet of *Eleven Poems* as the poet of *Pastorals*. Charles Williams claimed in 1930 that Blunden had "one great advantage—he does not stress and accentuate his own personality."[57] Stress consciously, no; display in a confessional way, no; but Blunden's is nonetheless a personal poetry—we find the man, and more often the actual man than an artful refraction of him—in each verse. A traditional figure in a turbulent time, he knew that in poetry "each fresh triumph spells some hurts and spurns,"[58] but he was comfortable in the imaginative house he built to echo with the voices of earlier poets. He sustained and supplemented a number of traditions in remarkable ways, even as he crafted his own song.

That song began with the land.

Chapter Two

The Field:
The Poetry of Nature

Reading Nature's Poets

Blunden's deep awareness of English verse convinced him that "poets live most on their youngest and least premeditated discoveries in the world about them."[1] He found keys to the work of Spenser and Shelley in their days in Kent and Sussex, just as he knew his own work was decisively shaped by the first place he knew, the Kentish countryside around Yalding, "a place beautifully environed with hopgrounds, cherry, damson and apple orchards, and rivers and ponds. . . ."[2] But the fact that Blunden, unlike many nature poets before him, did not get his living from the land causes some critics like Jon Silkin to find his relationship with it inevitably "less intimate" and the poetry produced by that relationship somewhat "literary."[3]

There is some truth in this, but unqualified acceptance of the argument that a nature poet must be connected to the land by economic necessity would cast disdain upon all English nature poetry except that written by such peasant wonders as John Clare himself. Certainly Silkin's point about livelihood could be applied with equal fairness to such "nature" poets as Wordsworth. What is important to isolate from his argument ultimately is that Blunden was about as intimately acquainted with nature as it was possible for him to be in his time—which is to say still a good deal more so than many poets who turned back to nature as subject matter during the early success of the Georgian movement. One has to beware, too, of Silkin's, and others', use of the word "literary." Blunden's nature poetry is indeed that. But that is not to say it is precious. Wordsworth or Keats might be said to have written "literary" nature poetry, too; they had to accommodate natural subject matter to poetic convention in the end, no matter how much that convention was modified, and earlier literature was drawn upon to assist in the task. And just as it is possible to have varying degrees of intimacy with nature, so it is possible to be either casually or profoundly aware of the *literature* of nature. Blunden's knowledge of that literature was great, and he would gladly acknowledge its direct influence on his own nature writings.

James Thomson, William Collins, William Cowper, John Clare—these and other nature poets who occupy less brightly lit parts of the eighteenth and nineteenth century literary stages, at least by posterity's ranking, were early and enduring enthusiasms of Blunden's. The list of poets in his war pocketbook, jotted in what seems to have been an exercise designed to keep a grip on his nerves, might have been written by him a half century later, so constant was his judgment.[4] His reading led him to believe that the poetry of the English countryside should be native in idiom and form, and direct in its observation. In Thomson's "The Seasons," he found, for example, that the "passage on the nightingale . . . mourning her stolen nest, would be more touching if we did not feel the ambition of poetic artfulness, after classical models, too clamant in it."[5] And yet, art must control observation. Even Clare "was, in a sense, never to know deep down what the art of poetry is—to espy that tyrannous judgment, that aesthetic economy. . . ."[6] Blunden could understand how Clare's inventory of nature's charms was like that of a lover looking at his mistress, but he knew that the resulting detail could be stifling.[7] If the precision of observation in Clare's poetry could be given a shape and structure—an "aesthetic economy"—an ideal for English nature poetry might be formulated.

Blunden's own natural learning and powers of observation were increased by reading more than just the poetry of nature. He also knew the popular prose writers who had observed the countryside. Too often, because of their once great proliferation, their books were "thrown aside like yesterday's newspapers," but Blunden was a keen student of many of their works, so much so that he could find "Ellis on Sheep . . . better than Ruskin on Sheepfolds." There was a solidity and vigor to their sight, thinking and prose, and they have been scorned by "professional" poets and literary historians at literature's peril.[8] Indeed, one could find an "antidote to idiocy and an inspiration for sound re-creation . . . [in] a farmer's ordinary, a scientist's lecture, or an eighteenth-century schoolbook."[9]

There was a glory, Blunden felt, in precise observation and recording of the everyday. This was as much a function of poetry as its visionary one. Nature will always provoke something, just by showing itself to the poet; there is no need for him to come to it with a plan. Nature must be viewed and respected for itself, before she can be called upon to give rise to any poet's self-centered considerations. Blunden thought that Wordsworth, for example, with all the power "descriptive and evocative and revelative of Nature" in his poetry, often condescended to it: "It is possible sometimes to mistake Wordsworth for the Creator rather than the created. . . ."[10]

There is power enough in the simple thing, by itself. Any poetic record of observation will generate some emotion. As J. C. Squire, one of Blunden's early patrons, remarked of Blunden's poetry, "It is not 'mere description.' . . . Feeling is implicit everywhere. . . ."[11] Feeling could arise, Blunden felt, from "a dull brown thicket, beside a gray-gorged river" as easily as from a rainbow, the thicket deserving just as many "Chances of Remembrance."[12] In "The Eclogue," a father quiets his son's feverish imagination, which has been dwelling on rushing winds and whirlpools, by showing him the quiet beauties worthy of quiet counting, by making him see "below calm trees calm waters gliding."[13]

Even the more decorative, histrionic poet of the earlier *Pastorals* knew that the water-fays, "The Fair Humanities of Old Religion," were not to be found "in the shining, countless ways / Of tossing, windy seas whose idle force / Is lost in foam," but rather in calmer, quieter spots, "[w]here small roach poise, mottling the brook's clear sand. . . ."[14] "Wild Cherry Tree," a poem written during the last year of the First World War, is also more poetically formulaic in its diction than most of Blunden's poetry, but it too is a good example of the constant sense of surprise and reverence which the simplest objects of nature called up in him:

> O the silvery cherry, the visionary,
>   Templed in dewy dim green pleasance
> Where moths flutter bloom-like—who shall utter
>   The shining wonder of her presence?[15]

The poet observes and records, but announces his own feelings in general, even apologetic, terms. The sense of wonder which the observations bring forth is communicated, but neither probed too insistently nor defined too sharply.

In attempting to define poetry through its effect on the reader, Blunden acknowledged a quiet community of poet, reader, and past poet. His own reaction, as reader, was not so strong as the famous spinal shiver Housman spoke of: "For my part I only hear a happy murmuring, which stirs in some recesses of the silent mind a host of delicious echoes, and it goes hard with the actual words of my poet's poem for an instant; but then I come back to his neighbourhood and to the significance of what he is uttering."[16] Supremely familiar subject matter is not a threat to, but the foundation for, this echoing community of response. In praising Robert Bridges's "Nightingales," Blunden warned young writers not to "seek for novelty of subject too labouriously."[17] Readers of nature poetry wanted, Blunden believed, a certain familiarity of expression, even in writers of special power and vision. Writing to Edward Marsh from Japan, he expressed his "idea . . . that some poets as Shelley do pretty well by dint of fearing no cliché, 'lovely forests,' 'purple light,' 'murmuring of summer seas,' [']sweet buds,' 'lush eglantine' &c. being part of his bait for beauty seekers."[18] Blunden is poking some fun here, to be sure, but the humor rests on what was for him a worthy truth.

The Mind's Eye

Before feeling can be experienced and expressed, before philosophical implication can be drawn forth, there must be a clear sighting. Some of Blunden's poems on animals provide the best examples of his precise eye at work. "The Pike" prompts thoughts of the dark side of nature's order, but the stimulation to such reflection is a carefully appointed picture of the action:

> Sudden the gray pike changes, and quivering poises
>   for slaughter;
>   Intense terror wakens around him, the shoals scud
>   awry, but there chances
>   A chub unsuspecting; the prowling fins quicken,
>   in fury he lances;
>   And the miller that opens the hatch stands amazed
>   at the whirl in the water.[19]

"The Poor Man's Pig" lives in a calmer world, but one whose elements are just as carefully placed for the eye to follow, one to the next:

> Already fallen plum-bloom stars the green
>   And apple-boughs as knarred as old toads' backs
> Wear their small roses ere a rose is seen;
>   The building thrush watches old Job who stacks
>   The bright-peeled osiers on the sunny fence. . . .[20]

The eye, Blunden knew, had to be satisfied before all else. One could not learn anything from an animal until one had seen it plainly.

Blunden's dismissal of D. H. Lawrence's animal poems is exaggerated, but instructive as to his own standards. Lawrence's "Baby Tortoise" fails for Blunden because of the vagueness of its adjectives ("alone," "small," "tiny," "slow"); Blunden is left "still looking for the tortoise."[21] Blunden's own animal poems are always best when he begins with his own eye; his attempts at animal monologues, for all their whimsical skill, are not particularly distinctive.[22]

One of Blunden's most repeated phrases was "the mind's eye"; he used it as the title of one collection of essays, and it recurs frequently in his critical discussions of other writers. One can make the case that his own poetic imagination, particularly in its contemplation of nature, was primarily a visual one. John Press of the BBC asked Blunden late in his career whether he had "been much influenced by the other arts, by music or by painting," and Blunden responded: "I think when I was told I was a rural writer I would rather have said rural painter, in my way. I don't know whether it is legitimate, though, for a poet to think he can paint in words. That's perhaps a fallacy."[23] Whether or not this connection of one art with another is legitimate, Blunden was well aware of the history of English painting and the extent to which other English poets had employed "painterly" technique. In *The Face of England* he hails a January morning of "the true British School, the constantly re-expressed treasure of roofs, and trees, and falling and rising grounds, grassland and ploughland, silver interstices of pool or brook, under a sky that can be an ocean in tumult or a shell of porcelain."[24] Writing about English literary studies in Japan, he digressed briefly about painting; the English landscape artists were especially admired for dwelling so often on the quiet side of nature—the side most fit for poetic celebration, certainly his own: "To me, in spite of a thousand adorations of other and more magnificent schools of painting, the British landscape artists both in oils and in watercolours have something of bewitching poetry and intimacy with nature which no others regularly show."[25]

Also a devoted student of Bewick and Cruikshank, visual artists of the landscape, Blunden felt that a talent for visual arrangement could aid those who tried to depict the land through words. By 1819, Shelley, in Naples, had had the chance to survey Italian painting, and the knowledge he gained was "sharpening his poetry, making him perfect and enrich the details. . . ."[26] A quiet canvas and a poem arranged with a calm, though sharp, eye were the most appealing to Blunden. At "Buxted":

we idled there
With verse of Wordsworth in our minds,

Not of his mightiest, deepest kinds,
But such as he when young devised
To paint the scenes his walks comprised.[27]

In "Triumph of Autumn," Blunden strove for the same lush effects
Keats achieved in his ode to that season, making special use of the deep
colors Millais used to paint the fall:

Vast is the triumph which at your behest
Will blaze abroad. The sun himself shall stride
With clanging pomp, bronze east to rubied west,
The moon sway wine-flushed after, lion-eyed
Star-companies form, tree-columns of glittering
crest
Uphold their rank in blue air. . . .[28]

The appointment of different components in precise relationship,
using punctuation to direct the reader's eye from one part of the picture
to the next, keeping metaphor to a minimum—this is the technique
practiced most typically in Blunden's quiet word-paintings of nature.
The first stanza of "Winter Ending" is composed in blank verse;
Blunden used this meter less frequently than any number of rhymed
forms, but it seems to allow sight even greater than usual dominance
over sound, and "Winter Ending" therefore provides a good illustration
of his visual method of composition:

In thin whirlpooly wind, birds are at work,
Running in couples, thrush and blackbird; crowds
Of starlings prodding through the chosen field;
The daw or crow stands on the old ewe's back.
Much gray and pale among, one gem of noon,
One brilliant pool, that summer will not see,
Lies girdled with such greenness that a snake
Might borrow glistening wildfire for his coat.[29]

But Blunden's skills in sound and meter were also considerable, and he
never attempted to compose free from their dictates. In his nature depic-
tions, Blunden was especially skillful at the slow, almost mournful, line:
two people looking "Into the Distance" hear voices "That come from
farm and road below the hill."[30] His skill at assonance was well developed. The last stanza of "The Poor Man's Pig" is exceptional in its
massing of unobtrusive but effective collections of short "u's" and "o's":

> Then out he lets her run; away she snorts
> In bundling gallop for the cottage door,
> With hungry hubbub begging crusts and orts,
> Then like the whirlwind bumping round once more;
> Nuzzling the dog, making the pullets run,
> And sulky as a child when her play's done.[31]

Country words, arcane and onomatopoetic, give their own appealing rhythm when strung together in his poems, or his prose: "The baaing was mingled with the flat clanking of a sheepbell, strapped round the neck of a wether who was battening monotonously on nettles."[32] J. C. Squire once privately admonished Blunden to strive for greater "variety of TUNE & appearance on printed page,"[33] and one might be tempted to say of Blunden what he himself said of Vaughan: "In metre Vaughan had one vital gift and no more: for iambic verse, and particularly for the eight-syllable couplet."[34] Blunden did achieve many of his best effects in exactly that form, as did his hero Clare in portions of "The Shepherd's Calendar." But if he could only occasionally vary his standard iambic rhythm, he could resort to varying lengths of line, from trimeters to fourteeners, to achieve any number of different results. He worked in many different rhyme schemes in his shorter lyrics, and was particularly adept at creating new arrangements of the sonnet. He remained, however, fundamentally satisfied with most of the staple English verse forms: "the great series of metrical inventions which tradition has already evolved is almost capable of supplying the main rhythm and cadence for any one of our new instances of poetic passion."[35]

He had a natural facility for versification that allowed his output of poetry to become as large as it did. He thought revision "a necessary evil . . . logic pretending to be magic. Those changes and recastings which occur in the original drafting are the only safe revision; the rest, at an interval, is a lottery."[36] He wrote Leonard Clark in 1964 that his "old way was mainly to fix on my text in my mind; it may have been the wrong way, & nowadays I fight more pen in hand for what may be the best expression."[37] That same year he told John Press that he could not have taken a poem through the many drafts that Graves would during the Boar's Hill years, and that, in fact, he "used to be rather conceited that [he] could write a poem straight out and leave it at that."[38] An examination of Blunden's extraordinarily neat manuscripts confirms this; "The Poor Man's Pig," for example, appears to have gone through only two drafts—the second different from the first by only several word choices.[39]

For all its facility, however, Blunden's nature poetry does not have the almost excessively readable quality one has come to associate with many Georgian productions. Some early pieces of Blunden's are marked by a coy or lazy kind of Georgian brush, but the "wood-fairies" of "The Unchangeable"[40] and the fish who longs, in "Perch-Fishing,"[41] for his departed mate, rarely dominate. Robert Graves has pinpointed the chief problem of most Georgian verse: through attempts to avoid Victorian pomposity of theme, as well as the wickedness of the 1890s, it "became principally concerned with Nature and love and leisure and old age and childhood and animals and sleep and similar uncontroversial subjects."[42] As time went on, the more perceptive critics began to separate Blunden from this movement, insofar as it was one. It has become accepted practice to set his work, along with Edward Thomas's, apart from the rest of the Georgians' as "a more genuine and satisfying pastoralism,"[43] and to realize that their links to the Georgians were more a matter of biographical circumstance than anything else.

But Blunden did not scorn Georgian verse, even long after it was out of favor. In *Shells by a Stream* (1944), for instance, he paid tribute to some of the "Georgian" aspects of Lascelles Abercrombie: "the glad lyrist now in orchards walking, / Now on high moors, and always friend of morning, / Curious and happy in the rural round."[44] The "amiable idolatry" of country life practiced by the Georgians, and their brave vision of a strong, simple poetry, were forgiven by Blunden because he knew that "the idolator had not yet travelled widely through the older poetry of England, and then, as Coleridge has explained, the voice of the new age is naturally enchanting to that age (if there is any life and urgency in the hour.)"[45]

The nature poems of the movement were, however, often flat and uninteresting. Harold Monro's "The Nightingale Near the House," for instance, is an overly abstract and delicate thing compared to what Bridges did, and Blunden admired, with the same subject—no matter how familiar it was, and no matter how distinguished previous poems on it were.[46] Sometimes Georgian attempts to be both "poetic" and straightforward all at once resulted in ludicrous combinations of the fey and the vulgar—such as the last stanzas of W. H. Davies's "All in June":

> Today, the fields are rich in grass,
> And buttercups in thousands grow;
> I'll show the World where I have been—
> With gold-dust seen on either shoe.

Till to my garden back I come,
Where bumble-bees, for hours and hours,
Sit on their soft, fat, velvet bums,
To wriggle out of hollow flowers.[47]

Those most genuinely interested in Blunden's work advised him not
to settle for this sort of thing. Sir Edmund Gosse wrote him in 1923:
"The laxity of the poets who are called 'Georgian' annoys me very much.
Most of them are satisfied to appear in public with slippers on their feet
and their braces hanging down their flanks . . . I want you to rise
superior to this sloppiness."[48] Blunden managed to do that through his
greater precision and more vigorous diction.

A list of "Poetical Reminiscences" he made in the 1930s shows
Blunden's sense of the leaders and fashions in poetry in his lifetime, and
contains evidence of one especially significant and salutary influence
upon him; there is the entry: "T. Hardy—HARD WORDS."[49] Early
in his career Blunden had his own "hard words" glossed, and some of his
mistakes pointed out, in a Society for Pure English tract by Robert
Bridges in 1921. To take one example: "*Stolchy* is so good a word that it
does not need a dictionary."[50] This was flattering early attention from
the Poet Laureate. The pamphlet shows that Blunden sometimes used
his rustic words in an artificial, academic way, but they were an
important element of his poetry, especially this early in his career, and
were usually used with skill.[51]

The effects of Blunden's migration to Japan on his "authenticity," his
particularly English eye, rhythm, and vocabulary, were surprisingly few.
Style, and for the most part subject, remained the same. Even when the
landscape observed was distinctly Japanese, Blunden caught its look and
mood with the technique already familiar to him and his readers. Some
poems written in Japan, like the three short ones collected under the title
"Moments" in the late 1940s, are really single, quick, delicate images,
and seem to show a Japanese lyric influence, but these are comparatively
rare.[52] From the "Far East" Blunden could for the most part honestly
assure the English landscape that he had not forsaken her: "Think not
your image in my breast / Was darkened when I sang my best / Beside an
Eastern sea." There, in the home of an "Oriental Giles" who "serves a
god much like your own, " he looked for and found mostly the same
elements of nature's calm and plenty that he had in England.[53]

The Japanese influence has been misinterpreted by some. Graves, for
example, insisted that Blunden, after having "risen to be the most
commended nature poet of the period," by going to Japan "sacrificed the

initial advantage that he derived from his country breeding. . . ."[54] The results were not so dampening as this indicates. They were closer to those pointed to by Antonio Amato. Writing about the importance of nature in Blunden's war poems, he argued: "There are two protagonists in the war poetry: the countryside and the soldiers. The countryside is that English one seen through the filter of the French countryside, in somewhat the same way that Blunden will later observe Western life through the lenses of the Japanese world."[55] It is true that feelings of exile in Japan, and later in Hong Kong, served to sharpen Blunden's love of England in a less horrifying way than fighting in France had. But the Asian "lenses," unlike the war ones, were removable; they functioned for the poems Blunden wrote while actually in the Orient, but they did not remain in place when he returned to England. When his real subject, the English countryside, was once again actually before him, he saw it as he did before the Japanese experience: the newer poems did not become comparative or markedly different in outlook. In the main his experience in Asia was neither so broadening nor detrimental for his poetry as one might expect it to have been.

The English Consolation

The preceding discussion of the descriptive methods and skills Blunden employed in writing about nature should not lead to the conclusion that he saw mere representation as the sole end of such poetry. Poetry's chief task in describing nature was to capture its spirit, to communicate those feelings it gave to man. The "course of the true pastoral in this country," Blunden felt, had something of "spiritual discernment" in it. Any English vision of nature was incomplete without that: *"The Tempest* is English pastoral at its ultimate pitch." The imagination which fails to court the spirit will fail in poetry. Tennyson's pastoral, "promising to combine all the reports of fine sense, and perception, and shadowy apprehension, drifted into a compilation of natural history jottings, to be thrust into his versification at a pinch."[56] Precise description alone may not convey that spirit entirely: it "leaves the one joy undefined."[57] As the poet describes one hill, the reader's mind may turn to a hill that is part of his own memory. The attempted conveyance fails.

Sometimes "the indirect excels" in the communication of the *"genius loci,"*[58] and the poet who is to have success with nature's spirit should be neither a mere photographer nor a philosophical goad directing his reader's thought insistently along any one path. When in *The Natural History of Selborne* Gilbert White describes a drought or storm, he "is careful not to theologise these for his readers. He paints the scenes, and leaves us to form our deductions."[59] The poet must respect both his subject and reader, allowing them their own parts in the shaping of the natural vision. In his biography of Shelley, Blunden quoted a rather breathless letter written by the poet from Keswick in 1811 to Elizabeth Hitchener, and commented that Shelley "fancied that the imported quasi-philosophical attitude was more impressive than the thing itself."[60] Simple cataloging and didactic philosophizing both had to be avoided in the poetic attempt to communicate nature's spirit. Blunden came closest in his own poetry to capturing the most essential lessons and moods he experienced from nature by careful selection of detail and modest self-expression.

The mood the poet brings to nature, Blunden believed, affects his reception of her image and meaning. When the spirit is healthy, nature's cyclical aspect is most likely to be celebrated. In "A Budding Morrow" Blunden expresses what was for him a typical relief:

> I who had drooped the last eve's hours
> To think the year forsaken
> Saw all the air bloom with fine flowers,
> And laughed to have been mistaken.[61]

He wants the world to retain its familiarity, to undergo no more changes than those seasonal ones mandated by the earth's orbit. He is unsettled by the sudden and unfamiliar:

> Dance not your spectral dance at me;
>   I know you well
> Along this lane there lives no tree
>   But I can tell.
> I know each fall and rise and twist;
> You—why, a wildflower in the mist,
>   The moon, the mist.[62]

The movement of the seasons allowed him, as he wrote in his diary during a crisis, to "live, as in all respects, for the return of spring."[63] In some respects his life and poetry can be regarded as an attempt to make the healthful rhythm of the seasons his own.

But for all his search for the serene in nature, Blunden did not fail to write of its darker, and even violent, undercurrents. He was not always, as Ivor Gurney once characterized him in a letter, "absorbed by lane-look."[64] "The Pike," for example, already cited, does not flinch from the sight of nature's own violence. And the moon in "Evening Mystery" also works an ominous effect: "Can she who shines so calm be fear? / What poison pours she in slumber's ear?"[65] On the mildest day one may find that Nature, along "human paths," has yet left room for

> An ambushed utter thing without a face,
> A death begetting
> On bright strength a defiled death-case.
> Strangest abetting![66]

English Poems (1925) contained what was by far Blunden's darkest nature poetry. In "Winter: East Anglia," "the cornered weasel stands his ground, / Shrieks at the dogs and boys set round, / Shrieks as he knows they stand all round, / And hard as winter dies."[67] In "Water Moment," "the dumb shoal shrieks, and by the stone / The silver death writhes with the chosen one."[68] The sun dries up a brook, "And in a day will strew with tiny bones / This universe dried into sands and stones."[69]

The sense of nature as a friend rather than something too distinct from man to be a comfort, grew up, Blunden believed from his own reading, only gradually between the Elizabethan age and the eighteenth century: "The recognition came late, and is as yet far from complete. . . ."[70] And should never grow to be so, he felt; part of a nature poet's maturity lies in the ability to recognize and deal with nature Tennyson called "red in tooth and claw." Keats's 1817 collection failed in parts, Blunden felt, because the "harder, darker side of nature, or the possibilities we know in the accurate knowledge of a bird's life, or man's self-seeking influence on the other creatures, had not yet appealed to [him]. His circumstances had not led him towards such thinkings."[71] Although Blunden's own temperament more naturally sought the calm and beautiful in nature, he remained open to the frightening side, almost as a duty, throughout his career. Writing to John Masefield in 1966 about the Royal Poetry award, he confessed that the "grotesques and macabres" of Ted Hughes were things he could only read "now & then" but admired for their "startling" qualities.[72] The violent was another strain of English nature poetry which Blunden embraced, and Michael Thorpe has been wise to note that Blunden's own "darker-toned nature poetry deepens his affinity with Hardy."[73] Part of that affinity was inbred, but more of it was the result of an uneasy obligation to the truth, fulfilled by traveling purposely against the grain of personality.

The most disastrous damage to the spirit or to poetry, Blunden knew, was an inability to feel nature's power at all, for good or evil. Blunden wrote of London fog in *The Face of England*: "He is deathly, but we are old enough to have seen strange shapes, and to keep our eyes open even in the worst moments. The real death is when impressions cease. Come, monster."[74] The violent outcroppings in *English Poems* are not the most distressing poems in that volume, either to poet or reader. Worst are those poems expressing an inability to respond to nature in any way. Wounded with a "strange perspective,"[75] he finds "Old Pleasures Deserted":

> Beneath this shroud of disrepute,
>   These scurfs and soilings, lay rich store:
> But creeping on, the shade of death
>   Has changed this air;
> Gaspingly I take my breath.[76]

He found his life "driven on, on, on / Like poor hare running till her heart is broken. . . ."[77] The volume echoes with pleas for an end to estrangement and a renewal of feeling, and often with an utter lack of confidence that such will come. "The Brook" is approached by the poet just as he did in better days: "But what dying fall, / What low ebbing syllables / Hear I now? what ghosts recall / Their shadowing piteous chronicles?"[78]

The ghosts are those of the war dead. The pain is real, not the youthful, self-conscious melancholy of the schoolboy poems, such as "A Song Against Hope," written before the Somme battle.[79] The war that physically destroyed the land of France and Belgium was nearly as cruel in its aftereffects as in its immediate violence. The attempt to regain confidence as an observer of nature, to trust once again that sensations would come and that the sights of nature would not be interesting just in terms of their suitability as war metaphors, became one of the prinicipal themes of Blunden's nature poetry after the war:

> I am for the woods against the world,
>   But are the woods for me?
> I have sought them sadly, fearing
>   My fate's mutability,
> Or that which action and process make
>   Of former sympathy.[80]

"The Recovery" of "temperate sense" was difficult, being often broken by torment and numbness.[81]

He called the countryside "the English consolation," and viewed all writers who could share it, from Coleridge to the Duchess of Newcastle, as literary kin.[82] Thanks to nature for her "healing power"—this, after the word-paintings and attempts to capture nature's spirit, is the largest and most accessible portion of his nature poetry. Jon Silkin, who has examined Blunden's nature poetry in terms of his war experience, maintains that consolation is really all the war left him to find in nature: "A belief in nature as a permanent repository of goodness cannot be fully recovered. A kind of religious disillusioning remains. . . . Nature may be consolatory now, but she is no longer man's preceptress."[83] Blunden would grudgingly admit only a part of this. Nature in a very real sense saved him during the war; he and it survived their battles with violence, no matter how shattered and defensive they became. However precarious that survival, he chose to believe that nature might ultimately lead man back to a better way. He would not close the door. If he remained receptive, some answers might get through:

> When June's white-throated warm convolvulus
> From the green hedge seems wisdom watching you,
> Gaze, gaze and gaze; here's chance harmonious;
> The old stone sunning by is watching too.
> Fear nothing, so you have not strumpeted
> The pride and essence which is yours and theirs. . . .[84]

This plea against his own "Resentients" is the final poem in the dark 1925 collection. As tentative as it is, it represents a faith in, and a willingness to fight for, a future of the spirit with the land. And if his own fight was never comfortably and completely won, Blunden came to reestablish his own "Deeper Friendship" with nature with some solidity. In *Near and Far* (1929) he declared a kind of victory:

> Were all eyes changed, were even poetry cold,
> Were those long systems of hope that I tried to
>   deploy
> Skeletons, still I should keep one final hold,
> Since clearer and clearer returns my first-found
>   joy.[85]

Nature was his "maker, mother!" Having "felt before the need her consolation," he did not abandon his hope that man could find his place in her.[86] He did not feel that the natural world had had her day, any more than he felt the poetry of nature had had its; he was amused by those critics of nature poetry who "saw the world in terms of men and women" exclusively.[87] The natural world remained at the center of every theme he attempted in poetry, not as mere decoration or metaphoric vehicle, but as a vital element. He could brook no separation of man and nature, regardless of what war and history were perpetrating. He had seen a world of men in nature—the village world in which he grew up; and this was to be not only one of his most important subjects, but his model for living as well.

Chapter Three
The Village:
The Poetry of Country Life

Man and Beast

When Blunden went into the countryside he looked for images suitable to his word-paintings of nature's own things: particular fields, particular streams, particular creatures. But man and man's creations were in the landscape, too, and the life Englishmen made in the countryside—a life different from any other—was as much a part of Blunden's poetry as the land itself. Ecology was not one of his words, but much of his nature verse is "ecological" in the largest sense. The delicate balance of man and nature was one of his principal themes. The life of the village, and threats to it, had been examined in English poetry from the early eighteenth century on, and Blunden's worry over the vulnerability of the village in his own century of accelerated rapacity extended the concerns he saw in the work of Gray, Goldsmith, Cowper, Crabbe, and others. He sought to capture, explain, and usually celebrate the life of the village, and to give warnings to a time that threatened that life as never before.

The farmer's life is by its very nature something superimposed upon a world without men, and a number of Blunden's poems express its unavoidable precariousness. There will always be "Misunderstandings" between men of the land and the land's even earlier inhabitants. In one poem, the well-intentioned man who spies the nesting wood-pigeon startles the bird: "he but looked and learned, / But to her frost-cold eggs she ne'er returned."[1] Elsewhere the poet asks the reader to "unriddle" a dream of fishing he had in which he was troubled by his own cruelty in performing an act that is merely part of the order of things he knows, the chain of being on which country life depends. There is a necessary violence running through the act from the baiting of the hook to the landing of the catch:

> I knew my prize, and fought my best
> With thought and thew—then the fight ceased.
> Sobbing I feared the quarry gone,

But no, the deadweight showed him on,
Slow to the mould I pulled the huge
Half-legend from his subterfuge.
And as he from the water thrust
His head, and cleared its scurf and must,
Two eyes as old as Adam stared
On mine.[2]

The relations between man and beast can be violent even on the most ordinary days. In *The Face of England* Blunden tells of witnessing the sawing off of a boar's tusks and of his wonder at the brutality of the act: "there he was, in hideous apprehension, entirely, so far as he could understand, at the mercy of a set of torturers."[3] In a diary entry made at Hawstead Place on 28 January 1930, he was "struck by the kind of faces that bloody-mindedness towards animals produces in humans," and warned that "Nature will not forego her revenges."[4] Decades later he advised men to treat kindly the "Wild Creatures at Nightfall":

No mains, no switches, hydrants, reservoirs
Command their lives, they make no Progress yet;
I hear sometimes, they stray beneath the stars
Into man's light, strange waifs! and there have met
The dead shot of that mind which made such light
Rather than trust the deep sweet soul of night.[5]

If country man is too casual or cruel in his predation of the beasts, to whom will he appeal when his own fragile world is menaced by the town, or war, or science? Blunden would have the larger and modern world find an example in country man's behavior toward the creatures over which he has dominion; he would have the world of the village be an ethical showplace: "Fair play itself has never been a fairer jewel than when it lay between a man and a fly or a bird."[6] There is a life to be learned, and a literature to be written, in those simple and honorable relations.

The Faces of England

When all is right with the village world, Blunden celebrates it. The work and the play of the country are sketched with the same hard diction and economic syntax one finds in the nature pictures. In "Gleaning":

Hard clucking dames in great white hoods make haste
To cram their lapbags with the barley waste,

> Scrambling as if a thousand were but one,
> Careless of stabbing thistles.[7]

"The works of woodman, grazier, pitman, thresher," are admired in economic terms for their usefulness and in poetic ones for the clear, musical relationship of sound and sense between each occupation and its name.[8] These men are, or should be, eternal. One can spy them after work, in their cottages or at "The Crown Inn," where "They like their clocks keep one same pace / While empires shudder into night."[9] On "Winter Nights" when work and trading are done, they will be at the *Bull* or going home, and then "the lovetalk, carolling, dancing din, / Are the heart's invincible law."[10] Long after Blunden's life was lived mostly in cities—Oxford, London, Tokyo, or Hong Kong—he continued to return to the villages to speak of their inhabitants with affection and hereditary pride. He never made them targets of condescension or scorn, something he felt the poet Herrick had done in the seventeenth century upon his return from London to the country, and which distressed him: many of the epigrams that poet applied to "Buggins, Truggin, Reape, Teage, Mudge, Tubbs, Raggs" and his other parishioners at Deane Bourne were, to Blunden, "dull, tasteless, and unnecessary."[11]

No activity better represented the village, Blunden thought, or was more fit for contented praise, than cricket. In the book of prose he wrote on that sport during the Second World War, *Cricket Country*, he made it plain that cricket was worthy of verse that was not only pastoral, but philosophical and consoling as well: "Lovers of the poetry of Keats must not dismiss me as unworthy of further association with them if I say of the cricket of my time that its groups and postures and borders are not unimaginable as pictures on another Grecian Urn such as he contemplated; or else I will attempt to convince them when the passing cloud of war leaves our greensward as golden as it used to be—sometimes."[12] Tom Fletcher, a boy cricketer who dies before he can be killed in the First World War, is the "Pride of the Village," a kind of artist who makes "his poems out of bat and ball." And the poet who elegizes him tells the boys who follow in the game that "Cricket to us, like you, was more than play / It was a worship in the summer sun. . . ."[13] The great cricketer Walter R. Hammond was such pride on a national scale, the Christopher Wren of the game in Blunden's paean, the interpreter of "[t]he game's delight, the infinite art, event and joy."[14] Cricket is, in Blunden's writings, almost a part of nature's own cycle. New cricketers are like flowers from the same ancient trees. A laborer watches:

the meadow is quick with the champions who were,
And he hears his own shouts when he first trotted
        there,
Long ago: all gone home now; but here they come all!
Surely these are the same who now bring bat and ball?[15]

Like so many things that appeared eternal to Blunden in village life,
cricket was treasured as a hedge against the invasion of modern vulgarity
and horror. In *Cricket Country* he admitted that it was an antiquarian
impulse which quickened his love of the sport even in the early days of
his manhood: "It arose like a ghost out of the ground, haunting this or
that stretch of short grass or pathway side, luring us to it without
question or anything but willing hearts."[16] It was no mere comic Tory
reflex that made Blunden see a threat to cricket as a threat to England
itself. On 6 June 1939, Seigfried Sassoon wrote him from Wiltshire that
he, Sassoon, was "organizing what protest I can" against the Ministry of
Transport's intention to build a road across the Heytesbury Village
cricket ground,[17] and two days later Blunden responded: "May your
efforts succeed: if the first don't, please dig a trench in the right place &
collect us to hold it. Really I should like to see actual resistance if so
idiotic a plan is put into practice."[18] He declared seriously in *Cricket
Country* that one could detect in Sassoon's successful captaincy of a
country cricket team "a parallel to his poetry, that part of it at least
which utters his sense of things natural and rural and their lasting
pre-eminence."[19]

    There is a chapter in *Cricket Country* called "Paint Me Cricket," in
which Blunden reflects on the tradition of cricket painting in England
and the reasons "why cricket can never be painted in its true light." The
painter might capture its "outer forms," but "that spirit of the game"
which Blunden observes in a farmer-bowler who lives not far from
Mulberry Hill "would not appear in any picture that Crome himself
could have achieved."[20] This has a bearing on Blunden's written depic-
tions, both in poetry and prose, of cricket and other events of country
life. He was well aware of the work of English genre painters and
print-makers and the relations between their art and poetry. Bewick and
Cruikshank ranked, according to him, with Hogarth: The "difficulty
of amassing the 'facts' and conjuring up at the same time the *genius loci*,
which has latterly driven poets in the several arts into strange postures of
perplexity, pessimism and 'revolution,' never occurred to [them], and
never occurs to us [their] much obliged servants";[21] the Japanese color-

print with its "exquisitely lighted glimpse of men, women and manners" also attracted him from his first acquaintance with it.[22] Blunden himself "composed" his rural scenes detail by detail, or, as he titled one of his essays on prints, "line upon line." J. C. Squire recognized his skill in this: "He sees every detail with acute clearness, but they are all of equal importance to him. They are important in themselves, not merely as contributions to a picture."[23] This skill is sometimes, however, limiting. Of Blunden's "scenes" containing more than one creature, house, or landscape feature, one could say what Blunden himself says of Constable's painting *The Valley Farm* in his poem "A Family Discourse": "Within is love, is birth, is death, / Gleam, shadow, desire, dust, wealth and wreath; / All quiet in the picture."[24] The inner life was something he captured only with difficulty. The components of the "picture" remain more autonomous than even perhaps Squire would admit is a good thing. Blunden attempted, it seems, to overcome this difficulty in *The Face of England* by enclosing a spirit of place in a mannered and less than usually concrete prose.[25] It is an impressionistic, mist-shrouded book of quiet moments—indeed, it might have been called *Undertones of England*. But his talents lay mostly in the direction of the particular picture.

The "Country Characters" in those pictures know as much as Bacon, or Coleridge, or the poet himself. They listen to a natural music that "[c]an summon a pure silence; end bad things. . . ."[26] They labor; in this is their happiness, and in this is what makes Blunden's celebrations of their lives in the spirit of the most authentic pastoral. As Renato Poggioli observed: "Manna does not fall on pastoral soil, and the shepherd neither fasts nor feasts but satisfies his thirst and hunger with earth's simplest gifts, such as fruit and water, or with the milk and cheese he gets from tending his sheep, which provide also the wool for his rustic garments."[27] In 1955 Blunden wrote Sassoon: "you know I still have 1 brother there [in Yalding], and he is able to quote John Dyer or Matthew Green, but is content as a labourer in his kind, and so is Hilda his wife. She goes into the fields, and knows what the world's about."[28] We see the men at a "Country Sale" as they are, and always were:

> The gathering grows
> With every minute, neckcloths and gold pins;
> Poverty's purples; red necks, horny skins,
> Odd peeping eyes, thin lips and hooking chins.[29]

Blunden's work may not be entirely free of the generalized Hodges and Ha'pences of poems like "Will o' the Wisp,"[30] but it is rich in individual character studies. The poet looks to these countrymen not only for his art, but for his personal renewal. Of "A Yeoman," he writes:

> This man that at the wheatstack side
> Sits drinking of the twilight air,
> This man's my friend, in him's my guide
> And guard against the traps of care.[31]

The early *Waggoner* and *Shepherd* contain Blunden's most remarkable studies of country people. The title poem of the first volume provides merely a glimpse, in five quatrains, of the waggoner as he moves through the countryside at dusk;[32] but "The Shepherd" is a rich and full portrait of a man and his work. The verse is careful pentameter, the diction solid even though smoothed with a notable talent for assonance, the tone almost hushed:

> The stubble browsing comes, and grand and grave
> Autumn in shadow swathes the rolling weald,
> The blue smoke curls with mocking stealth afield,
> And far-off lights, like wild eyes in a cave,
> Stare at the shepherd on the bleaching grounds.
> Deeply he brooks on the dark tide of change,
> And starts when echo sharp and sly and strange
> To his gap-stopping from the sear wood sounds.
> His very sheep-bells seem to bode him ill
> And starling whirlwinds strike his bosom chill.

Not only is he pictured for the sake of his striking, even stark appearance, but for his eternal nature as well. As the "dark tide of change" whirls like the starlings, he goes home with his tired dog to his fire and opens the Bible "[w]ith trusting tears" to read of the Shepherd Christ.[33] By the end of the poem this figure whose initial description had an exotic appeal has become perfectly natural, perfectly at peace; and the outside, new world, the "tide of change," has assumed the strange and sinister cast the poet intended for it.

The "Mole Catcher," also given in *The Shepherd*, does his work with a deliberateness and precision mirrored in the poet's style of rendering it. His trap is set:

> The bow is earthed and arched ready to shoot
> And snatch the death-knot fast round the first mole
> Who comes and snuffs well pleased and tries to root
> Past the sly nose peg; back again is put
> The mould, and death left smirking in the hole.

The mole catcher has his own morality and rules for dealing with nature—"moles to him are only moles," but hares, flies, and ants are spared, according to the dictates of necessity and feeling.[34] As David Perkins notes, "We may be inclined to draw a moral, but Blunden leaves that to us. His technique is typically objective."[35] The context of Blunden's other character poems, however, may provide a sense that the poet's own voice refuses to give explicitly in any one of them. The mole catcher on Sundays "[i]n the side pew . . . sits and hears the truth" from his vicar, just as the shepherd finds it in the Bible he keeps by the fire. The simple religion of the country people is as natural as their surroundings, although to an outsider it may be as much a "grand arcanum" as the strong oily scent with which the mole catcher attracts his prey—something "[f]ound out by his forefather years ago. . . ."[36] All the beliefs and ways which have been naturally maintained through the centuries and have become knit without self-consciousness to men's lives, are pointed to again and again, if only indirectly and incidentally, as saving ways.

These rural figures, who could so easily be shown as queer or merely picturesque, are limned into real people, elemental and important. The two "Almswomen" may live in a "doll's house" beyond the village, but they are as much a part of the way of the world as any of its creatures:

> All things they have in common, being so poor,
> And their one fear, Death's shadow at the door.
> Each sundown makes them mournful, each sunrise
> Brings back the brightness in their failing eyes.[37]

Only rarely are these men and women tamed into anachronism, such as when in *The Face of England* we are told that "Chaucer's people" live in Hawstead.[38] They are far more frequently living people with strong voices. They are not often given their own monologues to speak, but the poet allows us to hear their conversation amidst his description and narrative. There is not much of the Gothicism of Edgar Lee Masters in Blunden's rural pieces, which are usually portraits of living men at their work rather than autobiographical speeches by the dead, but the straight-

forwardness of the American's technique influenced Blunden's own
"personality" poems. In "A Poet's Death (1958)," he asked: "Where is
he / Who gave us once *Spoon River Anthology*, / Wherin he seemed to my
young mind to unveil / Of every churchyard every shrouded tale?"[39]

Blunden composed a few noteworthy prose character sketches. "Miss
Warble," for example, is about the frowsy tobacconist and former
comedienne who loves to forecast her death to customers. Blunden,
who was twenty-two when he composed her sketch, imagines: "The
Last Man will presently call on her for his last ounce of tobacco and, in
the petrified parlour behind the shop, among the dusty playbills and
autographed photos of a forgotten age, be permitted to admire her
miniature china piano, her ormolu timepiece in its glass mausoleum, her
family of assorted pets, and her raucous impersonations of the extinct
figurantes of Victorian music halls."[40] In *The Face of England*, Tatty, a
woman farm laborer, a sort of untragic and unbeautiful Tess of the
d'Urbervilles, is paid tribute in the form of clear, honest description of
herself and her lot: "So, there goes Tatty home again, with her hands
like a man's, in her man's boots, straight across those blackening
rain-swept fields. Hidden away in her greatcoat is a little doll, which
this night, by one candle's light (they are afraid of oil lamps), she will
dress for her youngest, maybe puffing a cigar she has by someone's
present."[41] Tatty, like Blunden's sister-in-law Hilda, "knows what
the world's about." In 1920, after the publication of "Miss Warble,"
Blunden's fellow Boar's Hill poet John Masefield wrote him of that
portrait: "It is a very complete picture. Someday you will have a book
full of such portraits as interesting & full of life as Earle's Microcosmographie."[42] It is unfortunate that Blunden never gave us his own
equivalent of that seventeenth-century book, for his early skill at such
sketches and histories is undeniable. In his account of Tatty, he called
half-seriously for a *Dictionary of National Biography* for those common
people left out of Sir Leslie Stephen's enterprise—what Sir Leslie's
daughter, Virginia Woolf, called, in the title of one of her essays, "Lives
of the Obscure."

In *The Face of England*, Blunden expressed his admiration of a hierarchy
in the village which gave each inhabitant his own place, and his own
right to respect. The landed gentry, if they treated those beneath them
in the scheme of things with grace and dignity, deserved to remain in
their grand houses; they too were a natural part of the landscape.
Their suburban replacements after the First World War did not please
Blunden's eyes:

Who now succeed? What demigods have we?
Who scraped the gilding from the family tree?
Ask of the roadhouse, try the bungalow.
Welcome, Squire Thenks-Chum and Lord Arfamo.[43]

"The Ornamental Water," like Yeats's "Coole Park and Ballylee, 1931,"
laments the passing "Of the great house on the rise through reed and
bough. . . ."[44] The war had destroyed the heart of the old system, and
with it, according to Blunden, some of the ideals and conditions which
had nourished artistic creation.

There seemed to Blunden little point in "democratizing" the lives of
those who worked the land. Their honest labor and closeness to nature
gave them more freedom than a reworking of the existing social order
could. The effects he saw of such a reworking both amused and distressed
him: "Zillah, aware of the democratizing age in which she lives now,
affects a superior manner. Bless thee, Zillah, how are thou translated!
But, as I watch her [in the teashop] manipulating a sickly sweet-cake
with a fork, I cannot help seeing her at home dividing her half-roasted
herring with her fingers, and replacing the tea-kettle on the stove for its
eternal stewing."[45] Reflecting on this same incident in his diary on 2
January 1930, Blunden found that this sort of "false progress and acting
may be seen in deeper matters."[46]

Country life and work itself were freedoms enough. Urban factory
workers would be better off even at the bottom of the landed system; the
season of hop-picking was proof of this. From his childhood on Blunden
took delight in seeing how the workers who came from London and the
northern industrial cities to help with the harvest were revitalized by
their work with the soil: "It must be a wonderful holiday, hop-picking,
for those who ordinarily have to fight for a little sun and air in mean
streets. . . ."[47] This may be a naive assessment of work that, as Blunden
admits, "occupies almost all of daylight,"[48] but the hop-picking celebrated in poems like "Jim's Mistake"[49] and "Storm at Hoptime" remained a kind of ideal vision for him, a time when the country could
rescue sons from the city: "Slatternly folk from mean, sad streets /
And crowded courts like rusty wells / Pick in that live and fragrant
air. . . ."[50]

The cricket season was longer than the hop-picking one, and the
playing field was where different classes might compete with honesty
and humor: "A much more powerful voice than mine has said something more on this: 'If the French *noblesse* had been capable of playing

cricket with their peasants, their chateaux would never have been burnt.'
So G. M. Trevelyan, in *English Social History*."[51] But here, in *Cricket
Country*, Blunden is expressing an ideal rather than what he knew of the
actual case in his own village of Yalding, which was not so simple. In an
unfinished memoir of his father, he recorded the presence of a "pseudo-
aristocracy" of the owners of large houses employing servants: "Between
them & the underlings was a great gulf fixed, & somewhere in that gulf
at differing levels anxiously revolved such strangers as the headmaster of
the Grammar School, the grocers & general dealers, the curate, my
father [a schoolmaster and the church choirmaster], & the clerks of the
post office, brewery, and station, with their displeased womanfolk."
There were two cricket teams in Yalding, "chosen on social grounds
rather than on merit. If the 1st XI composed of vicar, visitors, public
schoolboys &c. was a man short, C. E. B. [his father] was sent for. He
dared not offend by refusing, for the vicar & a retired Dr., besides being
desperately in earnest about cricket, were managers of the school. Many
games did C. E. B. play with the atmosphere of superiority to ruin them
for him."[52]

The Blundens themselves were part of the middle class that was
expanding in both country and city, and their ambiguous position made
a practice of *noblesse oblige* by those above them not quite satisfactory. In
Cricket Country Blunden was not telling lies or bending at the knee—he
knew very well how to dispatch pretensions to honor and sham codes of
conduct, and did so successfully in the excellent dramatic poem "Incident in Hyde Park, 1803," with its stupid dueling tragedy and the
operatic pomposity of the protagonists.[53] Rather, he was choosing cricket
as an unfortunate illustration of his ideal. Perhaps he felt the example
was true in the general; it was not in his own experience. That he could
put it forth at all shows the strength of the hold his vision had over him.

A Deserted Village?

Few subjects of English poetry have been more seriously debated than
the quality of life in the English village. The survival of rural life in the
face of threats from enclosure and industrialization has been the theme of
a whole subgenre of British poetry from the eighteenth century through
this one; Blunden's many poems concerned with the preservation of
village life can best be understood by first briefly exploring his own
awareness of the earlier poetry on that subject.

Although well aware of the bucolic poetry of the classical age and the
Renaissance, Blunden was more strongly influenced by the poetry of

rustic life which began in the eighteenth century in England—a poetry that came to eschew the ideal and mythological in favor of a depiction of the English landscape as it was in the present day. James Thomson and William Shenstone were among those poets who most pleased him in his youth. From the battlefields of the First World War he wrote his mother, asking her to send small editions of their work so that he could carry them with him in the trenches: "Somehow their placid and easy flight to my mind compares favourably with those rocket-like Shelleians who go up & burst."[54]

Blunden saw a fairly peaceful co-existence between city and country as having been the state of things in the early eighteenth century. He felt that even the poets of the latter part of that century, those after Thomson, had often exaggerated the dangers posed by the town; it was a good deal later, according to Blunden, that the real rapacity against the village began. Cowper might write that the cities "Attract us, and neglected Nature pines, / Abandoned, as unworthy of our love," but Blunden believed that, when Charles Lamb was born in 1775, "the town (in spite of Cowper) had not dispirited and depopulated the country."[55] So ghastly were the horrors of his own century that Blunden was inclined to see the differences between the threat it posed and the one the eighteenth century had as no mere matter of degree.

Unsure whether to claim Goldsmith as a calm ally in the cause of rural preservation, or to brand him, like Cowper, an alarmist, Blunden was confused in his appraisal of "The Deserted Village." Writing about Goldsmith's bicentenary, Blunden had almost unrestrained praise for the poem, but in *Nature in English Literature* he had found it too preoccupied with the economic threat: "The bittern and lapwing are made into mere signs of hard times, and no hint given that they are capable of anything but dullness. This is not the English pastoral."[56]

He found Crabbe's "Village," in an introduction to the life of Crabbe by his son, an "immature but disturbing" work.[57] Elsewhere he praised Crabbe as "an exact naturalist, and a happy one . . . [who] learned that his parish not only included the foul backyard and the seducer but also the charities, the charms, and endeavours of Nature apart."[58] Henry Newbolt noted that Blunden followed Crabbe in his use of the rhyming couplet in such portraits as "Almswomen" and "The Shepherd."[59] More important, however, was his borrowing of the realistic technique of character portrayal that Crabbe had used in *The Borough* and *The Parish Register*. Less brutal than Crabbe, Blunden nevertheless avoided sentimentality in depicting individual people—even if he sometimes drifted into it during group sittings.

As the scientific revolution joined the industrial one in the nineteenth century, the village was indisputably threatened, and Blunden admired those poets who continued to appreciate and understand its ways. Shelley and Hardy, both of them to become important subjects for Blunden, pleased him in this regard. In Shelley's *Oedipus Tyrannus*, he wrote, "we hear a master of ordinary [agricultural] affairs in almost every line."[60] Hardy "balanced his dismay at certain immense historical generalities" by continuing to respect the ordinary affairs of ordinary men.[61]

Conspicuously absent from Blunden's distribution of praise to poets who succeeded the "village" poets of the eighteenth century is Wordsworth. One suspects that, just as Blunden found Wordsworth apt to mistake himself for the Creator when looking at nature, he found him too much a creature apart when he looked at country men. The "Preface to *Lyrical Ballads*" has a tone that is more anthropological than would be to Blunden's taste, with its references to "these men" and their low "rank in society and the sameness and narrow circle of their intercourse. . . ."[62] Here the vitality of rural life is less important in itself than for the inspiration it provides the outsider, and this would naturally make Blunden uncomfortable. When attenuated to an extreme, Wordsworth's attitude led to such Georgian sentimentalizations of the English village as Frances Cornford's "Cambridgeshire" and Rupert Brooke's "Grantchester." Blunden's own village poems were seldom so devoid of sinew as those.

Blunden was not unaware of the dark side of life in the village of his own day. In any village of wallflowers, periwinkles, chestnuts, and grazing cows, there are still the unhappy:

> And for this black-clad ghost-like maid
> Whose cobbled shoes so wearily trace
> The dust, whose gaze on ground is laid,
> Whose steps are wounds—what happy place?[63]

In his poem "No Continuing City," the country schoolmaster takes a wife from the city and brings her to a life in the village which she is unable, and reasonably so, to appreciate:

> She shivered, and stood as if loth to be gone,
> Staring this way and that—on the watery road,
> And the inn with its arbour all naked and bleak,
> And the weir churning foam, and the meaningless oast;
> Till her husband turned back, and he stroked her
>   pale cheek.

> "O dear," murmured she, "must we go? but at most
> I shall never live here
> Above half a year."[64]

Forty years later she is still there. It is tempting to read this as the story of Blunden's parents; his father was indeed a village schoolmaster who took his bride, Georgina Tyler, away from London in the late 1890s.[65] But it is more important as evidence that Blunden knew there was in actual practice no easy complementary relationship between country and city, certainly not the ideal one Thomson had envisioned two centuries before. In *English Villages* he conceded a certain justice to Hazlitt, who "stated the case against our villages in a tremendous piece of accusation. His grievance was concerned with the character of the country dweller."[66] And he himself admired the character of Lamb, that ultimate celebrant of cities, perhaps above all others.

After war in France, Blunden's life was spent mostly reviewing in London, teaching at Oxford, and as a teacher and diplomat in the Far East. But he felt his spirit most at home in Yalding and similar places. "The Complaint," written after he had been away from the village for a decade, in " 'terrestrial war' " and " 'a world of men,' " is a lover's talk between the poet and the village that raised him. The village is both modest and clever, gently coaxing the poet back even though it " 'fit [him] for a mightier theme,' " and claims to be now too " 'small and poor' " for him. Despite everything, the poet feels he has come home:

> From school the hungry youngsters rushed,
> The caravan passed, the mill sluice gushed.
> "Dear,"
> I answered, "all my ways led here."[67]

Blunden was well aware of the perilous crossing made from the village to the town by poets like Stephen Duck, Robert Bloomfield, and of course John Clare, but his own position lay more naturally between the two, and he was bound to survive more easily than they.[68] Robert Graves saw the connection between Blunden and these earlier rural poets, but he made too much of it. In a letter from the 1920s, after Blunden's first successful work on Clare, Graves wrote to him from Islip:

You identify yourself with Clare because he represents to you the victim of village-life, unsuccessful in his attempts to win recognition in spite of the help given him by old Blues [graduates of Christ's Hospital] on the *London*. Where Clare failed you are out to succeed & thus avenge him. You have avenged him most miraculously & restored him to popular recognition. His ghost ought to have burned out its discontent. Now I hope you will lose a little of your sense of identity with Clare that you won't think of madhouses or Mary Joyces or of Clare's pastoralism as an end in itself.[69]

This psycholiterary interpretation of Blunden's early career has a certain appeal, but too eager an acceptance of it would obscure the main, and more simple, point that here was a man with roots in Kent and Sussex who deeply wished that England's country inheritance would be preserved; a man who could write to Edward Marsh from Japan that he had to go slow in his recovery from a recent illness: "I am reading White's Selborne but it is much too exciting";[70] a man who genuinely believed, as he wrote several years after that letter, in *Nature in English Literature*, that: "We need the virtues of Gilbert White and his Selbornian men and women very keenly at this moment of a threatened national character [1929]; and there is no obstacle to prevent us from close contact with them."[71]

Just as he felt Goldsmith had proclaimed the death of the village prematurely, he would insist that there was no reason, given good will and good sense, why the village should not survive in an even more dangerous time. He saw it as his responsibility to carry the poetry of preservation—that poetry from Thomson on which had recognized the continuing virtues of the countryside in the modern world—into the twentieth century.

"Modern Times"

His contemporaries, he felt, needed a lesson in respect for the past. In the preface to his biography of Shelley, he admitted that he was "not among those who think that the twentieth century with its eroded soil, 100,000-pound bombs, and cameras that cannot lie, is the flower of all time. . . ."[72] And in poetry he urged his contemporaries to "Think not too glibly" of the "Victorians" who preceded them: "Devise some creed, and live it, beyond theirs, / Or I shall think you but their spendthrift heirs."[73] They too had had their "Forefathers," whose achievements deserved the honor of continued use:

> Names are vanished, save the few
> In the old brown Bible scrawled;
> These were men of pith and thew,
> Whom the city never called;

> Scarce could read or hold a quill,
> Built the barn, the forge, the mill.[74]

But the twentieth century threatened those achievements. Walking along an "April Byeway," the poet noted:

> the old forge and mill are shut and done,
> The tower is crumbling down, stone by stone falls;
> An ague doubt comes creeping in the sun,
> The sun himself shudders, the day appals. . . .[75]

The technology that made the First World War so demonic had a peacetime rapacity, too. By the 1930s there was "a sort of civil war" in the countryside. Despite the survival of many rural beauties, "London, and the huge towns of the North and the Midlands, are able to crush with final force mile after mile of orchard and coppice. . . ."[76] The waters which excited so many of the reveries of Blunden's schoolboy poems were now being made filthy:

> by mysterious law each place
> Where Nature looks most gentle and glad
> Attracts the rubbish-dumping race,
> By whose refinement Nymph and Grace
> May walk in decent jam-jars clad.[77]

He will not say "To Our Catchment Board" that their work on his "first river" is wrong, but his distress is that the engineers seem to love the river "as a henwife loves / Some fated fowl, 'Regardez qu'elle est belle.' " He must count on the river to survive, because he has seen in it a sustaining spirit, "A certain permanence, a personality, / A liking almost for each opposition, / A willingness to make the best of things."[78] But there is danger to the waters everywhere, and he must make this worried wish "To Teise, A Stream in Kent": "May no man end / With short-seen plan or powerful greed / The centuries of your joy. . . ."[79]

The suburbanization of the land was just as lethal as the poisoning of the waters. In this century there was, he felt, someone worse than the eighteenth-century squire and his sham-Gothic ruins: "we have the figure who hovers behind the new 'avenue' to nowhere and 'drive' to the last bungaloid excrescence."[80] The "Chaffinch" tells a visitor that with the developments of the Housing Trust, and the " 'fancy gents' " who turn " 'Squandering Lane' " into " 'Hadrian Avenue,' " well, " 'times get worse for birds and worms.' "[81] Even the old Western Front, the essayist finds on one of his many return visits, has been sanitized: "The tourist sees parapets, treads along duckboards. These are not the parapets and duckboards that one knew on many occasions; there was a certain intimacy in a sandbagged buttress of earth, a wooden duckboard. The new exhibits are mere concrete effigies (they would have been useless!) lacking the natural touch."[82] Things at home are likewise varnished into uselessness: "Instead of going into the country for an adventure in primitive and pretty encounters, and a peep at an abundant round of skilful practical doings, from the wagon-shed to the wood-riding, we more and more assume the character of connoisseurs in beauty of architecture and of nature."[83] We have ceased, he felt, to look at nature naturally, fulfilling in the extreme the tendency he noted in Gray to make the landscape one thing and the watcher another.

He was not opposed to the placement of man's works in nature. On his early walks through the country he

> would'not haggle which were hers, which theirs:
> The church was brother to the chestnut-trees,
> The mossed bridge clasped his singing bride, gay
> Teise![84]

Even some of the industrial world's inventions could be accommodated—indeed celebrated. The railway is the most conspicuous example of these in his poems. It is usually a "casual Anglian train"[85] one sees there, one that has come to seem like an original part of the land. To his wife, Claire, he wrote in 1947: "Blessings on the railway for making homes for wildflowers even if we are hustled by too fast to see them properly."[86]

These remarks place Blunden in what amounts to a tradition of train celebrations, one which Robert Graves has traced from Wordsworth's "Steamboats, Viaducts, and Railways," through Tennyson's "Mechanophilus," and to Sacheverell Sitwell's "At Breakfast." By the twentieth century the train was, according to Graves, "not a 'monster' but a charming early-Victorian *objet de vertu* under a glass dome."[87] But this was not really true for Blunden, who admired utility and was generally uninterested in mere picture-book preservations. In his own address, "Man and Nature," for a Japanese audience, he commented sympathetically on Wordsworth's poem, and chose a passage from *Religio Medici* to append to the printed version of the address that included Browne's remark that " 'Nature hath made one World, and Art another. In brief, all things are artificial; for Nature is the Art of God.' "[88]

A genuine integration of man and nature was what Blunden hoped for. Earlier times had succeeded in this, the church tower and the treetops in a hamlet becoming parts of "the same solemn fantastic architecture."[89] He could marvel at the "Ornithopolis" of birds nesting in the architecture of Wren in London. Here was a true balance of man and nature:

> Never was covenant nor entente like this,
> Which still shall gather confidence and joy;
> Man's city chosen the birds' metropolis,
> Whole myriads taken with a fair decoy![90]

When nature creeps into the cramped city, there can be the restoration of a momentary calm and beauty, as in the rare city pastoral "London: A December Memory":

> The sun, the peace, the solitude
> Befriend the ugliest mass
> Of buildings, rarefy the crude
> Muddles of brick and glass.[91]

He was suspicious of new things, but not unwilling to make the best of some of them. The automobile provides a good example. It was frightening in its speed and numbers, but it too had its unexpected beauties: "after all, there are discoveries; the eyes of a dog in the beam of a motor-lamp are a beauty which our old horse-brake did not give us, and night has new trees to show."[92]

There is, however, a stylistic difficulty in many of the "preservation" poems. Although satire might sometimes be called for in his fight, it was not Blunden's chief talent, and when he employed it he did so awkwardly. Satire must provoke and embarrass, and some of Blunden's poems in this vein may succeed when read by those unfamiliar with the quiet tone of his later work. But those readers who are familiar with that tone may simply, and unproductively, resent the interruption of the accustomed communication between Blunden and themselves, so important a part of his appeal is the gentleness of his personality. The message may not get through. Also, there is sometimes in these poems a kind of excluding principle which seems to operate to no good end. In "Minority Report," it is "some," not "we," who are said to love life's

essentials, and the reader may wonder if he is being permitted a stake in
the battle. The poet addresses modernity:

> You will win; be not dismayed.
> Let those pursue their fantasy, and press
> For obsolete illusion, let them seek
> Mere moonlight in the last green loneliness;
> Your van will be arriving there next week.[93]

Blunden was a better celebrant than detractor, and one comes upon
his diary during the Second World War with relief, noting his attractive
remarks on the English character. He had grave reservations about a war
he felt was too enthusiastically embarked upon, but was still "singularly
moved by the number of good people one meets in England. Any adverse
judgments on our land must always be tempered by that. I love them for
their quiet, gradual emergence."[94] There was still the eternal dutifulness
and charm to be shown by the men Blunden often called "worthies."

Sometimes one wishes for more flexibility in a man otherwise so
gentle—a bit less insularity and a broader, clearer standard. Blunden
knew his own limitations when exposed to the new: in *The Bonadventure*
he apologized for a skimpy and not very vivid description of Buenos
Aires: ". . . I must admit that my scantiest notions of a town refer in
temper to the quality of its second-hand bookshops."[95] He would admit,
too, that his fondness for the used-book barrows, and "discoveries,"
leads him to a certain disproportion in his literary judgments and
rankings. This has a certain charm, but when it comes to the question of
what the modern world is to be about, Blunden offers perhaps too little
in the way of real vision or scheme. During the Second World War he
met occasionally with a group of friends to discuss ways in which a
reversion to country ways might revive the world after the war. From
this experience he edited *Return to Husbandry*, "An Annotated List of
Books dealing with the History, Philosophy and Craftsmanship of Rural
England, and intended to suggest alternatives to Commercialism and
Mechanization."[96] But it remains unclear to us how he believes his plea
"For the Country Life" can yield a new world after the war:

> The thing is only
> For us to bring to the wise ones in the field
> The strength so early revealed:
>
> And with those sunbeams,
> Those swallows under the eaves, and din

> Of cockerels and larks and cuckoos
> Let the battle for men begin,
> And I think we shall win.[97]

Here one needs more than lyric feeling: not a finely detailed and
Messianic program, or even a finely drawn philosophy, but some greater
expansiveness of thought. There must, one feels, be a more generous
attempt made to reconcile the past and present. In "The Survival,"
Blunden makes an unusual and graceful poem on such a theme; he
describes how the stones of an old house, now torn down, will make a
new road:

> Inheritance has found fresh work,
> Disunion union breeds;
> Beauty the strong, its difference lost,
> Has matter fit for flood and frost
> Here's the true blood that will not shirk
> Life's new-commanding needs.[98]

But such attempts are rare, and usually more grudging than this.

Hugh I'Anson Fausset too easily explained away this frequent unwill-
ingness to bring the new and old worlds together in Blunden's work by
claiming Blunden lived "in a world of his own, secure and at peace,"
oblivious to the challenge of technology.[99] Blunden's inner world was
actually not so serene, and he was hardly "impervious" to the challenge
the present presented to the past; the chief difficulty of his preservation
poetry is that he did not respond more realistically and sympathetically
to that challenge.

One feels that clearer grounds for saving things could emerge. Sometimes he seems to prefer old things simply because they are old. In *The
Face of England*, he candidly says he does "not mean to be indignant—
elegiac only, or perhaps a trifle boastful. It is something to have lived
out of one epoch into another."[100] And what follows is a catalogue of
things that have disappeared since his childhood. Later in that book, in a
discussion of the rectangular brick chimney, he uses the phrase "a
vigorous antiquity,"[101] and that seems to be a good name for his ideal.
One wishes he had brought that ideal into more frequent and sharp
focus; when he did give it expression, he made good sense. The ancient
bridges of Yalding, for example, were admired because they were "not
mere antiquities, but modern, essential workers in the life of the
village. . . ."[102] And if a mill was to be restored, then it should be made

to produce, not to be just a picturesque adornment to the "epicene and unlocal" house renovated by the "gentleman in a purple golfing suit. . . ."[103]

Sometimes he did admit the possibility of uniting the new and old on the land:

> I doubt not we shall have the land we love
> And its ancestral faith and annual round
> Flourishing by tried craftsmanship inwove
> With modern science, in one purpose bound.[104]

He could accept this "progress" in farming methods, if only regretfully. In Japan after the Second World War, he was pleased to see the "older way" of farming "continuing with great strength and usefulness."[105] But in poor Hokkaido, the touring poet and diplomat realized the need for modern methods and did not hesitate to call for them. His wish "To a Planner" is not that he cease work, but that he bring forth a "good plan" as soon as he can "win the general heart of man / To choose the golden age above the iron. . . ."[106]

These are his best moments and expressions on the subject, fine joinings of passion and sense, but they are sometimes blocked by the stubbornness mentioned earlier. Stubbornness and simple oppositions were inevitable in a poet's vision of the land. Blunden's Kent was his paradise of inspiration, a touchstone for all that lay beyond it, and the personal vision could not always be easily extended to the national or universal one. What in his own century science did to war, and war did to men, understandably made Blunden's own vision of rural England a more rigorous standard for reality than reality could bear. He did the best with science that he could. In a lecture on "English Scientists as Men of Letters" in Hong Kong in 1961, he revealed: "It has been my dream that Chaucer was one of our predecessors at Merton College, Oxford, once and even now a home of happy scientists, and certainly we have or had Astrolabes in the Library unless the Goya boys have been about."[107] But the relations between science and progress remained suspect, because of science's traffic with power and war. In 1954 he had confided to his friend and fellow book collector, Edward J. Finneron: "I have been moved by sundry writers who have urged that the English weather has been upset by atomic explosions. The day may come when all the statesmen will just say, No more of these leaps in the dark. There are none of the scientists I know who would want to *do* more than understand Nature and her laws before recommending any applications.

The new game is fantasy or comics, not due I suppose to science but to that queer goblin Power. You see my distraction is not yet over."[108] As he wrote in one of his late sonnets, "Modern Times," it is better to preserve the past in an age when "fierce year has bred fierce year . . . So let us live, and save, and in our turn bestow."[109]

He had left the life of the village almost half a century before these words, when he went off to the first war that made as much of machines as men. His experience in France created in him a state of mind wherein the field and village were things, quite literally, to which he must *return*, for his very survival. As Bernard Bergonzi has remarked in his book on the literature of the First World War, even though it is "an axiom of the modern literary consciousness that painful experiences are more intrinsically authentic than pleasant ones," Blunden "simply accepted the war as one of the basic data of experience that could not be evaded, even though it was always fundamentally less 'real' than the sights and sounds of rural England."[110] He carried with him until his end that sense of the greater reality of the land and the village as they were before August 1914. He tried to make room for the more benign parts of the modern world, and if he sometimes failed to do this well, it is difficult to condemn him, given his feeling that once we lose the ways of the country we will have lost all.

Chapter Four
Born for This: Blunden's War

To the Front

The urgency in Blunden's poems calling for the preservation of nature and country life is better understood after a reading of his war poetry, so much of which deals with the calamities he saw visited upon French and Belgian fields and villages as a lieutenant with the Royal Sussex Regiment from 1916–1918. He has in fact been read as the pastoral war poet, and the result has been an obscuring of his other, and perhaps principal, contribution to the literature of World War I.

Blunden is almost indisputably his generation's foremost poet of war-hauntedness, the one most concerned with war's aftertones as well as its undertones. He was among the very last survivors of the major war writers, and he performed active editorial and critical service as the custodian of their work and memories for half a century; but he fought with his own war memories in his poetry and prose longer than any of them. His war writing began in earnest with the Armistice. He wrote poetry while at the front, but some of that work does not survive; his poems from the summer of 1917, for instance, "down to [his] neat transcripts of 'ode, and elegy, and sonnet,' vanished in the mud."[1] His later war writings are chiefly about the continuing war he fought as a survivor. So important for him were the persistence, bendings, and painfulness of memory that much of his writing on the war is, in a sense, epistemological: how can he be sure of what he knows? He took one of the epigraphs to *Undertones of War* from Bunyan: "Yea, how they set themselves in battle-array / I shall remember to my dying day." Much of his war writing concerns the intractability of his recollections, the difficulty of shaping them into anything like a final understanding.

He was not yet twenty when he arrived at the front, and although he was a precociously gifted poet, his vision of the war was not so quickly complete as Siegfried Sassoon's or Wilfred Owen's. He wrote G.H. Grubb on 11 May 1930: "I was a boy when I went to France in the spring of 1916. That must have made all the difference in my reception of the consequent experiences."[2] He was well aware of the changes in poetry during the course of the war, and he knew why the poets had to respond in a new way: after the battle of the Somme, in which he took part, "War had been 'found out,' overwhelmingly found out."[3] But if the glory of Rupert Brooke's war sonnets could no longer be trumpeted, Blunden knew that the achievements of Sassoon and Owen, while he admired them, could not be his; he was left with fifty years to take the First World War beyond the brutal ironies of the first and the eloquent "pity" that had been the latter's proclaimed goal. He had to fight for his own particular clarity and vision of the war, and the resistance of that vision to solidification is the hallmark of his war writing. Time and again, both literally and in his "mind's eye," he returned to the Western Front; his war memories formed a field of still exploding mines, and the poems which resulted constituted, as he called a group of them in his 1930 collection, "Impacts and Delayed Actions." In a sense, he never came home.

Nature and the War

Thrust into "[a] whole sweet countryside amuck with murder," Blunden of course agonized over the cutting asunder of man's intimate relations with his natural surroundings, which had already been one of the chief themes of his schoolboy poetry, and it would have been easy and even logical for him to look now at nature simply as a forgotten standard from which men had fallen, an embarrassing contrast to their present brutality.[4] As Graves wrote in *Good-bye to All That* concerning his own poetry and Sassoon's: "We defined the War in our poems by making contrasted definitions of peace. With Siegfried it was hunting, nature, music and pastoral scenes; with me, chiefly children."[5] But Blunden's war poetry, whether written during or after the war itself, generally avoids any simple antithesis. In fact, so quickly did the war become "normal," as much a part of the men as their peaceful pasts, that distinction was a difficult task. A number of Blunden's poems, chiefly those included in *Undertones of War*, concern this difficulty. "The Guard's Mistake" is to walk "gamekeeper-like" across a country that, temporarily devoid of fighting, "lay . . . like a sabbath day." This "cowman now turned warrior" walks with "pace of comfort and kind ownership, / And philosophic smile upon his lip" until he once more, suddenly, is sent "scampering for his gun."[6] "Vlamertinghe: Passing the Château, July 1917" combines echoes of Keats's "Ode on a Grecian Urn" ("But we are coming to the sacrifice") with soldiers' diction to express wonder that the flowers near the château do not more closely resemble the blood of the battlefield:

> Such a gay carpet! poppies by the million;
> Such damask! such vermilion!
> But if you ask me, mate, the choice of colour
> Is scarcely right; this red should have been duller.

Elsewhere the mingling of peace and war is commonplace. No longer are the cows alone in the fields; there are "those brute guns lowing at the skies."[7]

Such confusion might be written with mere antiwar irony were the elements constituting the actual and the mistaken not sometimes reversed; genuinely peaceful country is sometimes misapprehended as treacherous. Sometimes the poet must apologize to field and village for wrongly thinking them deadly; sometimes, for brief moments, the calm is not meant to deceive. "La Quinque Rue" is addressed:

> O road, I know those muttering groups you pass,
> I know those moments shrill as shivered glass;
> But, I am told, to-night you safely shine
> To trim roofs and cropped fields; the error's mine.[8]

But the war changed nature permanently for Blunden. The pastoral world forever after prompted his memories of its destruction. The English countryside had been wounded just as surely as the French: after the war Wiltshire is difficult to look at because of the resemblance of its poplars, pools, and groves to the Somme country: "Resemble less, warm vale! that vale of tears. . . ."[9]

During the war, however, and despite any distortions, the sight of nature remained Blunden's most important *memento vivere*; therein he and his fellow soldiers could find confirmation of their humanity. In *Undertones of War*, Blunden tries to remember "that coincidence of nature without and nature within. . . ."[10] Nature was as fragile as man, and as capable of concealing destruction, but still the sun could rise in March and be greeted by birds with peals "as proud and fine / As though they had not dreamed of death all night."[11] The soldier left nature for the battlefield as he might leave a lover, someone whose memory only could be carried into battle like a talisman. But nature remained a world apart; in No-Man's-Land she was as dead as love. She could only be found behind the lines, and temporarily.

It was a holy respite nature offered the soldier-poet of World War I, but it was a more painful and more wholly separated rest than that given the soldiers of the past, particularly the literary past. In Book VI of *The Faerie Queene* Calidore regains strength in the world of Meliboe and

Pastorella, but Spenser, through Meliboe, makes clear that the fated task of fighting the Blatant Beast remains the real and honorable end; it cannot be renounced.[12] But the First World War was not a battle of heroes against a single beast; the beast had put on the armor of both sides, and one's task and fate could only be embraced with resignation. Blunden knew his fate, and in the ironic aubade "Come On, My Lucky Lads" he announced it: "It's plain we were born for this, naught else."[13] He can pray for "[m]anly" courage, and believe that "what you must do, do well. . . ."[14] But the end pursued is never a matter of glory or pride; it is the most dubious pursuit ever undertaken in arms.

Yet it could not be escaped, and one must do one's duty. Even Blunden, whose instincts were gentle, could not abide the fact that an Oxford proctor might escape his duty simply because "he knows more about Greek vases than any man in Europe."[15] Keats's "sacrifice" was now to be found near Vlamertinghe and not amidst the Elgin Marbles resting in London. Owen, to many including Blunden the most Keatsian of the war poets, was impatient with his hospitalization at Craiglockhart and longed to return to the men whose horrors he shared, and Blunden grew impatient with his own leave in 1918. They wished to be back at the front not to take part in a noble war but to bear witness to the slaughter with patience, love, and perhaps a kind of explanation.[16] Blunden loved his country and could write, in 1966, of the memorials in the Great Church of the Holy Trinity, Long Melford, as forming "a sad yet proud note on the history of England and the patriotism and sense of duty which have so frequently demanded brave endings by land and sea around the world."[17] But it is always in sadness more than pride that he writes of the Western Front. The slaughter of "our German cousins," written without irony, was a matter of fate more akin to Hardy's ideas of that force than Spenser's.[18] By the spring of 1917, before his service in the third battle of Ypres, Blunden was angry about the war but resigned to his own part in it. He had written his father in 1916 that he had "the saving gift of knowing, *I am playing the game*. . . ." But by the following May he knew only that it "is a crime to waste such wonderful cricket weather" in battle.[19] This was no greater game. War was not an amplification of his beloved sport; it was merely a travesty of it. Let cricket be, in itself, heroism writ large: in a later war, when Blunden wrote his book on the sport, he told this story: "A classical scholar of my acquaintance, who has been if he is not now among the names that count in his field of studies throughout Europe, often tells me that he has ceased to find much pleasure in the poems of Homer: he cannot now endure the cataloguing of heroic carnage in those hexameters."[20]

Since the task of war is no longer heroic, the soldier-poet does not seek inspiration in nature; he merely seeks escape—albeit an "escape" into a world more real than the battlefield's. The two worlds must be separated for sanity's sake; they require different men. During the year of the third Ypres battle, Blunden wrote in "Bleue Maison":

> Now to attune my dull soul, if I can
> To the contentment of this countryside
> Where man is not for ever killing man
> But quiet days like these calm waters glide.[21]

This mood could not hold. During the war itself circumstances shattered it, and in the fifty years that followed memories darkened its colors. Just as Vlamertinghe was too perfect—there the war had almost made nature and the country world artifacts, to be seen with a museum-goer's gaze—Gouzeaucourt offers a "Deceitful Calm"[22] and the fields near Richebourg St. Vaast in May 1916, with "[s]uch beauty neighbouring so much slaughter," offer the most ephemeral comfort.[23] The soldier must not be deceived into a belief in the permanence of what can only be a respite. But that does not lessen the need to impose the illusion for a while. When the soldiers held a party "At Senlis Once":

> How they crowded the barn with lusty laughter
> Hailed the pierrots and shook each shadowy rafter,
> Even could ridicule their own sufferings,
> Sang as though nothing but joy came after![24]

These places are holy to the poet, if only for giving him and his comrades sleep; Martinsart Wood, where Blunden was camped during the Somme battle, could only offer the consolation of its "skinny trees / And unmossed clay," because the war had violated it. But memory gave it sanctification for whatever shreds of peace it offered in its wounded condition:

> Thus to me in the vale of years
> Holy almost and serene
> Martinsart Wood appears
> May you be fresh and green
> Dear coppice, when Doomsday nears![25]

Blunden's poems are as concerned with this violent natural suffering as they are with what is inflicted on the soldiers themselves: Nature suffers as hideously as man, and Blunden paints that suffering in human terms and imagery. In "The Zonnebeke Road" the stones flinch in the wind, and the mutilated trees "fang" the ground.[26] So intertwined are the terrible fates of nature and man that a battered tree on a hill near Ypres is said to look "like a cross, but such a cross that there no bleeding Figure / Might hang without tautology."[27]

But the "coincidence of nature without and nature within" is still not so complete that the tortured earth does not exist as separate evidence of and comment on war's horrors. Physical nature's eternal and cyclical aspects are more ancient than man's, and this war, more horrible than any before, is even more presumptuous in its efficient killing of the flowers and fields than in its murder of men. Yet the natural world still manages a cry of sympathy for the men who are laying waste to it. "The Trees on the Calais Road" weep, as does the rain at "Third Ypres," as a chorus of mourners for the passing army. "The Ancre at Hamel: Afterwards" continues to weep in the haunted poet's memories years later; its crying waters swirl into his heart.[28]

The field suffers in a unique way: "although you may rebuild cathedrals against the clock neither zeal nor reparations will induce nature to throw up a hurried but gigantic colonnade of elms."[29] But the peaceful creations of man in the natural order, the houses, churches and barns, are also wounded and feel "human" pain. The poet addresses the soul of "A House in Festubert" which now houses guns instead of men and women at their dinner table:

> It hived the bird's call, the bee's hum,
> The sunbeams crossing the garden's shade—
> So fond of summer! still they come,
> But steel-born bees, birds, beams invade.
> —Could summer betray you?[30]

The spiritual and physical sufferings of the natural order as expressed by Blunden are more than "pathetic fallacies"—Ruskin's term for the artistic attribution of human qualities to natural phenomena. His expression takes its grandeur from the strong influence Hardy's *Dynasts* had over him. The Chorus of the Years in Part 3, Act VI of that drama express feelings of horror about the ordeal inflicted on nature's smallest creatures as the English and French armies march to Waterloo; the coneys, swallows, and moles are chased by cavalry and artillery. In his biography of Hardy, written at Merton College during the early days of the Second World War, Blunden took note of this aspect of *The Dynasts* without noting, as he might have, that it was he himself who extended this unique part of war writing to the Great War.[31]

The Style of the War Poetry

Most of Blunden's war poetry, both immediate and retrospective, is written in a calm, meditative style: the horrors of the war lurk amidst the gentle beauties of his language just as the guns and corpses were sometimes stumbled on unexpectedly in the fields. The imagination at work is again primarily a visual, or painterly, one. This is particularly true in the "delayed action" poems, wherein memory—the mind's eye—organizes itself in pictures. In "Rhymes on Béthune, 1916," the poet wonders at his desperate urging to record the way two sisters gave him lodging: "I cannot *see* them now, I grieve / To fail in this."[32] The italics are Blunden's.

Blunden's style and diction can vary given his particular wartime subject. "Into the Salient" makes use of a modern rapid-fire "imagistic" approach:

> Sallows like heads in Polynesia,
> With few and blood-stuck hairs,
> Mud-layered cobble-stones,
> Soldiers in smoky sheds, blackening uniforms and
>   walls with their cookery;
> Shell-holes in roofs, in roads,
> Even in advertisements
> Of bicycles and beer;
> The Middle Ages have gone to sleep, and woken up to
>   this—[33]

Diction is a mixture of the poetic and the colloquial in his "Rhymes on Béthune, 1916": after a night of "serene sweet-valenced sleep," it is a pleasure to "see a church not yet a wreck, / To enter the bank and cash a cheque. . . ."[34]

And yet most of these war poems have as their style a graceful, even stately, meditative one that recalls much of Blunden's nature poetry. Here, however, the introspection and subjectivity are greater; many of the poems take the form of a dialogue between the poet and himself. The older man may question his more youthful soldiering self, or, in the course of war, the part of consciousness accustomed to battle may question the part that has not yet fully come to believe the end of peaceful days. The soldier questions and admonishes the poet most forcefully in "Premature Rejoicing":

> it's a shade too soon
> For you to scribble rhymes
> In your army book
> About those times;
> Take another look;
> That's where the difficulty is, over there.[35]

Frank Swinnerton has noted the more gentle nature of Blunden's poems compared to much other World War I poetry: "Blunden is capable of savagery only to blasphemers against his literary gods."[36] It is true that Blunden's "counter-attack" on the war was neither so violent as Sassoon's nor so pitiful as Owen's, but this was because his gifts equipped him for a different mode of opposition. He made use, in his poems about the war, of the calm, understated style he had already developed for his pastoral poetry. It took on a more ironic tone and quality, certainly, but Blunden did not force his protest into an explicitness and stridency he knew he could not, given his own temperament, sustain. He wisely used his particular talents. D.J. Enright has written: "In the more successful War poetry, the style capitulated to the subject-matter; in the best of it, and predominantly in Owen's work, the style was *in* the subject-matter."[37] This statement can be applied less productively to Blunden than to some of the other war poets. The war directed his style along a more ironic path, but it did not overwhelm it; there is a greater consistency between the styles of his war poetry and his other work than there is, for instance, between Sassoon's war and peace poetry.

The task of the poets of the First World War in finding a suitable style to express a new kind of horror was not an easy one. There was no real "antiwar" tradition in English poetry. Blunden, who was to become the most learned of the war poets, searched for such a tradition in vain. Whatever glimmers of such sentiment existed were drowned by the heroic tradition. He found in the eighteenth and nineteenth centuries contributions "against the god of war" by Cowper, Leigh Hunt, and others, but still nothing like a tradition that an educated soldier-poet could take to the battlefield like a second nature.[38] In addition, the new fusion of soldier and poet called for a different kind of war poetry; and, other than the very ancient, there was little previous war writing that had come out of direct experience for the World War I poet to draw

upon. Even the biographers of Shakespeare, whose war writings were
revered by Blunden, "have failed to discover his army identity disc."[39]
The poets of 1914—1918 had to begin a new unheroic tradition for their
antiwar sentiments. There were almost no models: in his book on Henry
Vaughan (1927), Blunden wrote that "Abel's blood" gave that poet "a
place in that most honourable and perhaps smallest anthology of all, the
anthology of poems protesting against war."[40]

Rupert Brooke and Julian Grenfell, writing in the pre-Somme days,
had tried to sustain the heroic tradition in new circumstances. Blunden
did not scorn them. In 1930 he wrote: "We shall be liable to vain-
gloriousness if we now blame too earnestly the young soldiers of 1914
and 1915 who with their delicate and unreflecting stanzas failed to paint
war as it is. They were not experienced, and, at a time when the country
needed their sweetness, they gave it."[41] Indeed, so strong was the heroic
tradition that Blunden's own war poetry was sometimes affected by it: it
may not be into the "cleanness" of Brooke's noted phrase ("as swimmers
into cleanness leaping") that Blunden's "Infantryman" leaps, but the
last stanza of that poem contains echoes of Brooke's war sonnets: "You
smiled, you sang, your courage rang, and to this day I hear it, / Sunny as
a May-day dance, along that spectral avenue." But this is an exhausted
heroism, resulting from "ironic orders."[42]

Sassoon's enormous impact on the writing of the war was keenly
felt by Blunden, who later wrote that Sassoon was "the first man
who . . . described war fully and exactly. . . ."[43] In 1919 Blunden
sent Sassoon two of his own early books of poems "With gratitude . . .
for your great efforts throughout the war to bring the ferocity of the
trenches home to a public more disturbed about rations than Passchendaele. . . ."[44] The two became lifelong friends, and there are inevitably
echoes of Sassoon's ironic tone and familiar diction in Blunden's own war
poetry. In "Third Ypres" the soldiers are said to have " 'paid the bill' ";[45]
in "The Zonnebeke Road" one should "see old Stevens" and "Go ask
him, shall we win?"[46] While soldiers listened to the "Concert Party:
Busseboom," "men in the tunnels below Larch Wood / Were kicking
men to death."[47] Here is the unquiet closing that was so devastating in
many of the war poems of Sassoon and others. Blunden's "The Prophet"
uses colloquial commentary on the florid prose of an old guidebook to
Flanders to achieve an unusually brutal, and one might say Sassoonian,
irony:

The fields,
Our witness saith, are for the most part small,

And "leases are unfortunately short."
In this again perceive veracity. . . .[48]

But these are echoes and exceptions; they do not form the main stylistic line of Blunden's writings on the war.

Blunden also paid tribute to Owen, and one can detect the stylistic influence of that poet as well; Blunden's "The Welcome" has certain narrative resemblances to "Disabled," for example; and the humanity of "Strange Meeting" is echoed more strongly with the passing decades by Blunden in pleas for the recognition of the humanity of the Japanese and Germans—whatever the war. But Blunden's war poetry and prose remain less relentlessly "pitiful" than Owen's. For all of his awareness of the tragic nature of war, his poetry of recollection is less likely to depict individual soldiers as butchered victims than to celebrate their memories, and their acts of courage and kindness, in the same careful and gentle way that he celebrates old books. One cannot imagine Blunden showing the English he met on leave pictures of wounded soldiers, as Owen, according to the now familiar story, is supposed to have done. He would have applauded the intention of such an act, but he would not have been comfortable with the technique. So in his poetry he tries to convince in the quiet style that came unforcedly.

It is a style closest perhaps to such muted poems of Isaac Rosenberg's as "Returning, we hear the Larks" and "Break of Day in the Trenches." In "Third Ypres," "a score of field-mice nimble" scamper among the poet and his wounded companions in a shot-up pillbox. The poet clings to their regard much as Rosenberg let an unmenacing rat steady him: "(these / Calmed me, on these depended my salvation)."[49] Even though Rosenberg apparently had plans to write of the war in larger terms,[50] his self-questioning and personal poems show a shy and profoundly unmartial man trapped in a wholly inappropriate task, just as Blunden called himself, in the final words of *Undertones of War*, "a harmless young shepherd in a soldier's coat."[51] Those poems are probably nearer to Blunden's than any other war poet's.

Peace and Memory

What most sets Blunden's work apart from his comrades' is, however, his lasting preoccupation with the task of writing about the war. Sassoon believed, according to Jon Silkin, that Blunden was the most "lastingly obsessed" of the war poets.[52] Sassoon himself eventually concentrated on his religious poetry; Graves, another survivor, turned his hand to many projects unrelated to the war. Blunden, of course, did so as well, but the war remained a crucial part of his poetry until his death. As the years passed, his grappling with the subject of war became the subject itself; he examined war-hauntedness as much as war, and the ramifications of this inquiry were felt in his nature and philosophic poetry as well. In a poem called "The Aftermath," he wrote:

> Time has healed the wound, they say,
> Gone's the weeping and the rain;
> Yet you and I suspect, the day
> Will never be the same again.[53]

At every decade of his life he turned inward and backward toward the war. In *Cricket Country* (1944), he admits that his memory "seemed to undertake a burden for life during the War of 1914—1918—a case which must be far from unique";[54] and in a manuscript recounting of a dream, on examination paper from Hong Kong and presumably from the 1950s or 1960s, he wrote: "War dreams have been part of my life for over forty years. . . . I was looking out of the window, high over the square; and others were. On a sudden cords or coils of purple or blue-grey were there on the blue sky, and coming down to our world; and beauty mixed with terror was my impression."[55]

A.S. Collins is incorrect when he says that "Blunden's war poetry gives the impression of fulfilling Wordsworth's definition of poetry as being 'emotion recollected in tranquillity.' "[56] These war recollections were as often as not frantic, and would have been escaped if possible:

> Accept that when the past has beckoned,
> There is no help; all else comes second;
> Agree, the way to live
> Is not to dissect existence.[57]

He addresses his murderous recollections: "Memory, *et tu?*"[58] He prays to an angel to give his mind, traveling backwards, strength and fidelity to the truth, and, after that, deliverance: "And from that wayless saeculum of despond / O, can you lift to the flashing heights beyond?"[59]

Peace, the years between the two world wars, is viewed as if it were nothing more than the respite celebrated in the bucolic war poems:

> It's all the same. I thought the war was done.
> We'll have to hurry, the Battalion's gone.

> *How on again?* Only an Armistice.
> I thought my nerves weren't quite so bad as this.[60]

The war, with its "lost intensities of hope and fear," is more vivid than peace: "the charred stub outspeaks the living tree."[61] The ironic inability to enjoy the fields that comforted him in war when they have returned to their peaceful state is his special pain. But he pleads with himself and the world for patience and does not lose faith in the countryside's ultimate healing power.

The guilt of having survived the slaughter runs through this poetry of memory. In "The Watchers" he uneasily imagines that he will hear a sentry's voice when he dies, asking his name as St. Peter might.[62] But the dead, "Their Very Memory," can also bring relief: "to think of them's a fountain, / Tears of joy and music's rally."[63] So much pleasure does Blunden find in remembering the troops' selflessness that he must express added guilt over celebrating those "lost intensities" of the war years. He asks, in "Illusions," forgiveness for praising the stark beauty of trenches in moonlight.[64] And in early poems like "Clear Weather," and late ones, such as "Picardy Sunday" and "Over the Valley," he can celebrate, however difficult it is and with whatever reservations, the gentler memories of the countryside and comradeship.[65] He never stopped commemorating his fellow soldiers who "died in splendour, for they claimed no spark / Of glory save the light in a friend's eye."[66] There was some good and decency to be found yet in memories of the carnage, and it had to be written of. Writing Sassoon from Japan in 1926, he expressed admiration for that poet's "To One Who Was With Me in the War," which worried that good memories might drive out the bad, but offered a plea for "us retrospectors" in their celebration of the friendship they felt from others and the effectiveness they sensed in their own actions.[67]

Humanity was not displayed solely by the recruits; the officers had their fine qualities as well—and Blunden is nearly the only war poet to give them such credit. Sassoon's poems excoriating the staff, such as "The General" and "To Any Dead Officer," are well known; Graves put the attitude simply: "Trench soldiers hate the staff and the staff know it."[68] With Blunden it was otherwise, largely because of the benevolent influence and command of Colonel G. H. Harrison, who remained a friend for almost fifty years, continuing to correspond with the young "Rabbit" who had served under him. Harrison is celebrated in *Undertones of War* as the man who "put life" into his troops, and in a number of Blunden's poems for his good sense and faithful command.[69] Blunden especially admired this man's ability to put the war behind him, to achieve a real peace, to return to his garden, at war's end, where "contentment only thrives, / And the long misery of the Line is dead."[70] Harrison's gift was for remembering the virtues his troops displayed in the midst of hell; he wrote to Blunden of the Somme in 1952: "What times! yet I wouldn't have missed them for worlds. What good chaps those were & how highly tried."[71] Officers are praised in Blunden's poetry for showing the same *noblesse oblige* that he admired in the landed gentry: at the Southdowns battalion reunions he takes pleasure in "the voluntary, sweet and accomplished courtesy" he observes flowing in both directions between officers and men.[72]

The decline of this war spirit in postwar Britain, and the return to rigid class distinctions and manners, is deplored in such poems as "II. Peter. ii. 22: 1921," wherein England returns, like the dog to its vomit, to "Slyness" and "Quarrel," abandoning the "heights which crowned a deadlier year."[73] In "Some Talk of Peace—," Blunden openly preferred the gentleness displayed behind the lines to the "cold designs" of the more conniving and selfish years of the peace that followed.[74] The finer spirit declined; on 4 January 1930, Blunden recorded this incident in his diary: "The driver of the taxi-cab . . . refused to attempt our lane, called it 'wicked,' and so forth. Twelve years ago this man was probably forging ahead with a lorry through the genuinely wicked mud-tracks of Ypres. But we are all much lazier, and older."[75]

Undertones of War

"[A]ll the tiny circumstance of peace," it is apparent, could be viewed by Blunden in terms of the Great War. That war was more than a matter of battle; it was an entire way of life, with its boredom, intimacies, hilarities, and private fears—in short, its undertones. These were the things Blunden wanted to convey in the prose work that is arguably the greatest book of the war. *Undertones of War* was his most comprehensive attempt to deal with his sad hauntedness, and it waited until ten years after the war to be written. He made a first, unsuccessful, attempt which "although in its details not much affected by the perplexities of distancing memory, was noisy with a depressing forced gaiety then very much the rage."[76] It was not until his years teaching in Japan (1924—1927) that he found the right time and mood for his book. He wrote G. H. Grubb: "In Japan, my sense of loss and eyelessness became stronger, the first year there being of course productive of long periods of loneliness, though later on I discovered many springs of hope and sympathy. I also had some *time* now & then,—& so I began to picture the past as well as I could in words. (I had deliberately left all my old notes in England, and wrote without the awkward means of checking my memory,—on the whole, this was probably good luck.)"[77]

The result was a quiet, even ghostly, book whose prose is distinguished by stateliness, archaism, understatement, and gentle levity by turns; the author can be both self-consciously poetic and matter-of-fact. There is a sense of intimacy between the experience and the writer so strong as to be almost strange. H. M. Tomlinson perceptively described *Undertones of War* as a book written "by a ghost for other ghosts. . . ."[78] While its gentle qualities make the book accessible to the unscarred reader, one senses that Blunden is speaking foremost to the dead and haunted. When he writes, for example, "let us be getting out of this sector," he is not addressing the reader.[79] He stops to ask his comrades at Ypres: "do you remember me yet?"[80] They are the ones who would understand; others, perhaps not. Blunden interrupts his war essay "The Extra Turn" (1931) to say: "I do not know quite why I am telling my reader these things. . . ."[81] The reader himself sometimes wonders at the selection of detail in *Undertones*; the presence of the dead often explains things.

In his "Preliminary" to *Undertones*, Blunden explains that one of his reasons for writing the book was that his poetry could not incorporate the facts and details of his war experience that a book of prose might, but his prose narration remains poetic in the sense that it is still more selective and less time-bound than a conventional autobiography's.[82] It is always the undertone he is trying to catch: "Do I loiter too long among little things? It may be so, but those whom I foresee as my readers will pardon the propensity."[83] He wrote in the sonnet "Values": "It is my chance to know that force and size / Are nothing but by answered undertone."[84] It is the smallness of certain experiences which lends them, paradoxically, their significance; the emotional life went on unexpectedly, in the trenches, and hearts remained pure. There are fine portraits in *Undertones* of comrades like Doogan and Worley to substantiate this goodness, and one wishes for more of them. Blunden's talent for character-sketching, already remarked upon in discussing pieces like "Miss Warble," was largely neglected by the writer himself in the course of producing his enormous body of work.

As in his poetry, Blunden in *Undertones* is more concerned with understated sorrow than bitter irony. "So the attack on Boar's Head closed, and so closed the admirable youth or maturity of many a Sussex worthy."[85] This is offered in sadness, not as savage mock-heroism,

although Blunden does admit he may have been "too young to know
[war's] depth of ironic cruelty."[86] A more sharply toned memoir, such as
Graves's, might be more entertaining, but it is certainly less rich in
feeling. Blunden wrote Sassoon that Remarque's *All Quiet on the Western
Front* was "devoid of a sense of anybody's good or evil except three or four
self-confessed rascals,"[87] and that Graves's "self-importance and cold use
and slaughter of others" in *Good-by to All That* "ruin the possible solace of
a personality."[88] If he quarreled with Graves's book, he would, however,
have understood Graves's statement that his own first attempt to render
his experience in fictional form was done "stupidly";[89] in a later piece on
English war literature Blunden wrote that the "first requirement in a
literary work is feeling," which is obtained in war books by exploring
"the secrets of literal experience."[90]

How that "literal experience" was best transformed into a new war
literature has been the central question of the criticism that followed
it. J. Middleton Murry wrote Blunden that "those who were not at
the front are probably the best judges of whether an emotional effect
has been created by a poet."[91] Was the soldier unable to objectify his
experience sufficiently? John H. Johnston makes the argument that,
with the exception of Herbert Read and David Jones, the war poets
were unable to transcend the personal lyric and develop a literature
which gave the war its proper significance: "a tragic event which is
understood only in terms of personal misadventure ceases to be tragic."[92]
While admiring Blunden's work, he feels it is too much limited by its
concern with the nuances of his own ordeal. Blunden told his BBC
interviewer in 1964 that *Undertones of War*, with its "Supplement of
Poetical Interpretations and Variations," "adds up, as I meant, to a
sort of long poem. It varies, of course, in topics, but the uniting
argument, if there is one, is that war is like that and ought not to
happen."[93] Johnston would question there being a uniting argument,
but one must wonder why it is so important that Jones's "*In Parenthesis*
has much more in common with *The Battle of Maldon* than, say,
Sassoon's *Counter-Attack* or Blunden's 'Third Ypres.' "[94] Sir Maurice
Bowra is more correct when he writes: "Modern war provides no
material comparable with that of the *Iliad* or even of *Henry V*, and the
poets have to take it as they find it. Their record of what they found has
its own tragic distinction."[95]

The intensely "personal" literature they left behind is full of concern
for, literally, armies of men. This makes their poetry very different from
the main development of the lyric from the Renaissance to the present; it
is not as intensely self-preoccupied as some critics might have it. And

when the concern is with the self, that often gives it a special power; to read of Blunden fighting as a "harmless young shepherd" at Ypres conveys the enormity of the catastrophe indirectly, but with great poignance.

Sassoon and Blunden exchanged letters about Johnston's book after its publication in 1964. The first admitted that he had not actually seen the book but expected that "he works his professorial thesis about epics too hard";[96] and the latter wondered: "how could we have got a bit more formal control &c just when a shell came into the aid-post?"[97] These poets did not choose the forms they worked in without thought. As early as January 1917, Blunden was writing home about the unsuitability of this war for epic treatment: "I wish I could weave together all the moods and manners that I see out here, and make the epic of the age. But chivalry is not the atmosphere. It is all routine, a business with plenty of paper credit."[98] Sassoon's George Sherston recalls watching "an exhausted Division returning from the Somme Offensive. . . . It was as though I had seen the War as it might be envisioned by the mind of some epic poet a hundred years hence."[99] But Sassoon could not live a hundred years hence, and he too chose to render his war, for valid reasons, in "personal" terms.

The Literary Sentry

Blunden carefully followed the war poets' individual and collective reputations in the decades after the war. He edited Owen's poems in 1931, and in the early 1950s he edited the work of the troubled Ivor Gurney with special care and sympathy. There were also a number of introductions to the inevitable anthologies; he was willing to write them, but he worried, in letters to Sassoon, that the "war poets" were being unfairly perceived as a school instead of as individuals, and that the attitude of the public to such poetry was determined by shifts in politics. In the 1930s at Merton he saw his students neglect Owen's poems for the more overtly political work of W. H. Auden, C. Day Lewis, and Stephen Spender, and he was distressed that they would not take the same comfort the older poet continued to offer him during the decade Auden called low and dishonest. In the sonnet "To W. O. And His Kind," he wrote: "Your witness moves no Powers, / And younger youth resents your sentient youth."[100]

The unique horror of the First War was bound to diminish for a generation that was immediately afterwards eager to return to peace and later preoccupied with threats of a second war. As early as 1922, a

reviewer of *The Shepherd* complained that some of the poems in that
volume were "just bits of ghastliness, making miserable without any
justifiable reason."[101] On his clipping of this review Blunden underlined
this last clause and drew three question marks in the margin. In a
booklist on the war that Blunden helped draw up in 1929, he called
attention to the already present "danger . . . that the horror and crime
of war are being transformed into a glib axiom, a generalization which
may not work at the hearts of the new generation."[102]

He was not devoid of hope at the beginning of the 1930s. In his
opening Clark lecture on Charles Lamb in 1932, he said: "The knell of
war has been rung, if I perceive rightly what is in the consciousness of the
coming race, by mere obsolescence, rather than through the arguments
of experience."[103] But these hopes were steadily sapped in the next seven
years. Blunden continued to believe desperately in the need for peace, at
almost any price, and he was increasingly isolated from his fellow writers
who viewed him as too innocent; politically he was, but there were few
men less innocent of war. Blunden visited Germany in the 1930s, and
was particularly close to his German sister-in-law Annie, and he was
distressed that the essential goodness of the German people was being
lost in the public's perception of Hitlerism. He wrote in support
of a proposed educational exchange between Oxford and Göttingen,
which Oxford turned down, in the *Times*, and E. M. Forster responded
privately: "You fear that Oxford's abstention may be political. I expect
it is and don't see how it could help being, and her acceptance would
have been political also. Germany has chosen to make every relationship
political. . . ."[104] This was a typical feeling; the new war and Blunden's
resistance to it even strained his friendship with Sassoon, who wrote
him in 1940: "you & I have never had a shadow of a disagreement
between us yet. But it's no good. I *can't* be tolerant about the Nazi
aggression—or their treachery & ruthlessness."[105]

As the war approached, Blunden spoke out against nationalism and
conflict in such poems as "An International Football Match," "A Window in Germany," "About these Germans," "In the Margin," a plea for
the common Japanese he loved, and "Exorcized," which celebrated the
Munich pact as the last real hope for peace: "The meeting of four men as
friends unhorses all the ancient fiends. . . ."[106] In the preface to the
volume in which the poem was collected, he said that he could not
foresee the later "mischief when [he] wrote the verses, and many of [his]
friends who may afterwards have changed their minds were for the
moment pleased with what [he] said."[107] Reprinting the poem was an act
of some courage.

Waiting for the war was as painful to him as the horror that came, this time from the skies. Blunden, who admired the ideas of passive resistance both Shelley and Owen expressed directly or implicitly, could do little more than watch helplessly from Oxford as the world reeled once more toward self-destruction. No one could fail to be moved by the diary he kept during the fall of 1939. On the sixth of September he is "haunted by T.H.'s reply, when someone pointed to his optimistic conclusion of The Dynasts: 'But a stirring thrills the air' &c. He said, 'I could not have written that today. Why? The Treaty of Versailles.' " Failing to see the moral rightness of the war against Nazism, he writes: "My one real concern with the War now—for I do not stand with those who think Hitler is the sole cause of human happiness or otherwise—is to see it end."[108] He cannot but "recall the battlefield of . . . 1917. It is not the horror of dead men, exactly, that persists; it is the total drabness, the homelessness, the slowness. Everything was dead & damned."[109] He was tortured by what he felt the world should have seen as a simple choice between peace and slaughter: "I set down all these matters, and I could set down more, because I am an ordinary Englishman of modest position, of simple family tradition, and of an exacting patriotism. My country means much to me, and I do not like to see her driven by want of intelligence, and at the bidding of inferiors, into a devil of a mess. Neither do most Germans."[110] Blunden was to have lectured, at Christmas, in 1939, on English humor—in Hamburg.[111]

But "the hideous thing / [Was] loose again. . . ."[112] Life went on, and usefully, for Blunden. He sought comfort in the things that had always solaced him in nature and country life. He contributed to pamphlets calling for a return to husbandry, and what he thought would be a resulting return to sanity, and, as always, he did his duty: teaching military map-reading at Oxford. He read *Poems of this War by Younger Poets* in 1942, and the careful craftsman was alive to the new verse imperatives of a new war: "All the polishing in the world would not increase, indeed would impair, the fresh and significant appeal of these songs of emergency."[113]

There was a merging of the wars in his imagination. His diary on 5 March 1940 records a battle dream: "Which war does this dream refer to?" He returned with urgency to themes he never wholly abandoned. In *Shells by a Stream*, he wrote again of nature's consolation in war in such poems as "A Patrol" and "The Boy on Leave"—he wished him the same comfort and respite he had found a quarter-century before.[114] But nature is again being wounded, and is this time " 'past tears.' "[115] She is during this war more a world apart than ever. In poems like "A Prospect of

Swans" and "Dovedale on a Spring Day," he retreats into nature more fully than ever before.[116] And still the other war comes back; a member of "The Halted Battalion," he is among the most tortured of those at home: "We who draw / Picture and meaning are the dreamless, we / Are sentinels of time while the rest are free."[117]

The "postwar world," whose label he must have found anomalous, brought the nuclear bomb. He protested in "H-Bomb" and "A Sonnet after Listening to BBC News, 12 November 1963."[118] Sassoon shared this new agony. On 18 February 1955, he wrote Blunden about a newspaper's telephoned request for his reaction to the hydrogen bomb: "When actively reminded of this thing (called out of the library to answer that question—think of it, weep for it, dissolute Man) one almost feels one's sanity none too assured."[119] There were also the new national alignments, but Blunden refused to believe that politics should stand in the way of common contacts. "At the Great Wall of China" in the 1950s, he understood that the new age's sentry was still a boy "[t]orn with sharp love of the home left far behind."[120]

War was his intimate companion for fifty years. In his sixties he would still return to the Western Front. His memories went back there continually. On 14 November 1961, he apologizes to the aged Harrison for sending his "old letter" of war memories.[121] But he never lost hope for the possibility of a better world, and he retained a romantic faith in the healing and visionary powers of poetry. Shortly after John F. Kennedy's assassination, he wrote his former pupil Paul Engle: "We must be patient, and we have not done wrong I think to believe that poetry has a great part to play still in civilising mankind."[122] This, despite a half-century of public and private agony.

Chapter Five
The Sum of All:
The Poetry of Ideas

The Philosophic Mind

Critical categorization of Blunden's poetry has been restricted largely to the terms "pastoralism" and "war poetry." His name is not usually associated with what might be called the poetry of ideas, even though his large body of work contains as many essentially "philosophic" poems as nature or war pieces, indeed probably more. But he was singled out for his talents in describing nature and war early in his career, accumulating much praise before he was thirty, and the labels stuck. In 1923, J. C. Squire, as a leading spokesman for "Neo-Georgianism," wrote that Blunden "speculates and reasons hardly at all; his philosophy or his search for a philosophy is to be guessed; he does not even incite to the guessing. He is content to recount his loves and leave the argument to someone else."[1] It was above all the precision of Blunden's portraiture that was noticed, almost wholly to the neglect of his more abstract work. When he collected his poems in 1930 he expressed pride that he had been recognized as part of the pastoral tradition, but also "the desire that those who take up this book will not altogether skip those pages which are non-rural. They were derived from unstrained, general feelings."[2]

The few times he essayed definitions of poetry itself produced results which probably, by their breadth, surprised many of his readers: "Poetry in general is an attempt to pass beyond or else to peep beyond the outward and seemingly solid structure of our physical being, and therefore some of its exponents have thought that it might replace religion and philosophy."[3] The verb "to peep" is the most important one here. He was always dubious about the possibility of achieving orderly philosophical systems and realized that it was the province of "[c]ountless English poets, not of the order of Dante or Milton, [to] have told of some flash of that beauty beyond all beauty, wisdom beyond all wisdom, which Dante 'stedfastly pored upon.'"[4] "Flashes," moments better given expression in the lyric than in the longer poem, is a good word to use in characterizing his philosophical insights and poems.

He was a poet of plain things, but many critics have failed to notice that these plain things were often springboards toward more complex reflections. He should in fact be seen as an example of those imaginative people who, he said, "first discern their large world in and through something very simple."[5] He could look deeply into his rural world, and had a right to resent such remarks as T. Earle Welby's that his poetry usually consisted of "loving or surprised inventory" of nature's gifts without reflection upon their relation to each other or to man.[6] Kenneth Allott was much closer to the mark when he noted that "'human unease is hinted at in much [of Blunden's] verse which at first would appear to be purely descriptive.'"[7]

It is the apparent tranquillity of the subject matter which provoked Blunden's larger reflections that sometimes deceives a reader into looking at no more than the skillful portraiture mentioned earlier. Blunden never deprecated a poet's attempts to probe the secrets of the universe; he was a sympathetic and often perceptive commentator on the philosophical successes and overreachings of Shelley's later poetry, for instance. He was, however, unable to believe that the ordinary world could not provide the material for far-reaching speculation: "In respect of human life, Blake looks beyond it with a certain tyranny; and we rebel quietly, since he could have responded in his pictures to so much of its various abundance. . . . Is not life 'worthy of the Muse'? But Blake replies 'Fourfold vision,' or so."[8]

Blunden devoted large parts of his poetry to expressions of his ideas about death, time, love, religion, and what might be called life itself. These poems are almost invariably lyric expressions, flashes of thought conveyed in an orderly style. Basic "positions" emerge from a survey of fifty years of his writing on each of these questions, but there are shifts of mood and feeling. What might be called not too neatly a "consistent inconsistency" is the pattern of his lyrics in each of these areas. His intellectual poetry is marked by the often searched for and debated quality of poetic sincerity; a personal voice and tone, rarely transferred to any persona, are almost always detectable. The earnest, sometimes desperate, quality of his search for firm answers and values may come as a surprise to those who have viewed him as a pastoralist, but it should not be surprising to those who remember the persistence of his attempts to make sense of the war which opened a nearly unbridgeable fault between his adolescence and manhood.

Memento Mori

The war forced Blunden to look at death repeatedly and in its most brutal and sudden forms, but even before he went into battle he had sensed death's part in the particular rhythm of village life. In many of his poems death is viewed as a presence lurking, perpetually, undramatically, in nature or the hamlet. Margaret Willy has remarked on Blunden's frequent use of war imagery in poems not specifically about the war, something Blunden himself noted in the preface to his collection of 1930, but he rarely gives death a martial, screaming air. More often it is simply an ominous, brooding thing, frequently resting in the water. In "The Midnight Skaters" it lies beneath the surface of the pond; in "The Subtle Calm" it is below the deceptively calm surface of the sea.[9] In "What Is Winter?" the poet tries to convince himself that winter is merely a word, that the spirit continues to live; but even so, death "is no more dead than this / Flower-haunted haze."[10] It is an evergreen part of the landscape.

The men of the country know its violent comings and goings. On a hot spring night at the alehouse, when the sky is rattled by "Sheet Lightning," the talk turns to sudden death, by drowning, in a storm, or of "Many a lad and many a lass. . . ." The talk becomes gayer when the weather clears; there is a return to ribaldry and complaint. But on the way home:

> Joe the driver stooped with oath to find
> A young jack rabbit in the roadway, blind
> Or dazzled by the lamps, as stiff as steel
> With fear. Joe beat its brain out on the wheel.[11]

The cryptic "The Last Ray" seems to describe a suicide in a farmhouse during a storm; and it is sound country wisdom to know that "Timber" will make coffins as well as housewares.[12]

Blunden noted in *Votive Tablets* that as early as the writing of Gray's "Elegy" the old ballad-maker's terrible images of death were being replaced by more misty and romantic ones; and the twentieth century had turned to the scientific and rational view: "The grinning Monster with his arresting finger-bones is gone, and a chemical law or evolutionary confidence is our usual substitute."[13] But Blunden himself could still find an arresting recognition of death's presence, often and forcefully, in stark country circumstance.

After leaving the battlefields of the Great War, Blunden married Mary Daines and began to raise a family. But death suddenly entered his life once more: his baby daughter Joy died in the summer of 1919 when she was little more than a month old. Blunden never wrote of the cause of Joy's death, but part of a letter from Osbert Sitwell to Blunden, dated 6 September 1919, reads: "I can't say how much I feel for you both in your sad loss. I should like to see the Milkman who sold the milk tried for murder."[14] Joy's father was not yet twenty-three. For forty years Blunden tried in his poetry to understand and reconcile himself to this death, just as he continued to speak of and to the ghosts of his fellow soldiers. The peace he made with her passing was every bit as uneasy as his tenuous reconciliation to the losses of war.

In an early one of these poems, which are too nearly completely concerned with the survivor's state of mind to be called conventional elegies, the poet refuses to be weighted with sorrow as he makes his way to his daughter's grave on a beautiful April day:

> This peace, then, and happiness thronged me around.
> Nor could I go burdened with grief, but made merry
> Till I came to the gate of that overgrown ground
> Where scarce once a year sees the priest come to bury.

But he cannot, particularly in this Easter season, refrain from wanting to hear from her spirit: "But the grave held no answer, though long I should stay; / How strange that this clay should mingle with hers!"[15] A few years later, alone in Japan, he took "A 'First Impression' (Tokyo)" and delighted in the sounds of the playing children, realizing there were millions of them in the world, "so kind in this / Is nature. . . ." But at last he still "saw a ghost, and lacked one child."[16]

Michael Thorpe is correct when he remarks that "For There Is No Help In Them," in *Retreat*, is "emotionally satisfying . . . finely balanced between feelings of loss and acceptance."[17] "Finely" in the sense of tentatively, precariously. This is the mood of most of these poems. The balance is indeed so "fine" that Blunden must write the same poem again and again, as he must write his war verses over and over, to be sure that he can cope with changes in mood, be honest about them, resist the temptations toward easy solution, mere palinode. During the Second World War, he takes a "Winter Walk" and thinks of someone else who died too soon. Love and nature console him, but this peace cannot remain whole. When he marvels at the eternal "ease" of the birds, several stanzas before the conclusion of the poem, he realizes he is contemplating a

> Fine-drawn illusion! still my heart
> Chills with the truth I know,
> That all created joy must part
> And the very brightest go. . . .[18]

These lines are more memorable than the consolation celebrated at the close. The solace is temporary; the grief, if its outcroppings are intermittent, is never likely to be banished permanently.

It was Blunden's great fortune to raise a new family when he was well into middle age. A new daughter, Margaret, is introduced to his memory of Joy in a poem written a quarter-century after the latter's death:

> we bring
> A second self with whom your span
> May round, with Margaret now you can
> Make fun of things, feed, call and sing,
> Tease, tantalize, adore, bewitch.

Heartfelt as these final lines of the poem may be, their nature, one realizes, is tentative, nearly desperate. The opening lines of the poem have a force the final ones lack:

> My darling, what power is yours
> To make me weep, after such years;
> For twenty-seven years at least
> Are gone since your brief coming ceased,—
> And still you force my hopeless tears
> And still your fate dwarfs all my wars.[19]

The reference to "all my wars" makes the reader familiar with Blunden's other verse conclude that this is the essential feeling, the one that has endured and will continue to do so, and to be skeptical of the final lines, whose catalog of verbs is weak, an attempt by the poet to impose his will on a situation that he cannot control for long. Any one of the Joy poems, or, indeed, almost any of Blunden's poems on death, time, love, or religion, will evoke substantially different feelings from a reader if it is read in the context of Blunden's other work rather than as a single lyric. The individual poems frequently end with a kind of resolution; the corpus presents a tentativeness that more accurately represents the poet's vision. Thorpe, in discussing "Joy and Margaret," says that "poetry often obeys mood and the mood [here] is true enough."[20] But a reading of "Children Passing," which follows "Joy and Margaret" in *After the Bombing*, sheds light on Blunden's awareness of the need to *manipulate* his moods in order to keep distress from becoming too great. Its light verse rhythm and diction almost belie the central idea that the growth of children makes for an infinite series of deaths. The poem frankly embraces a temporary dishonesty: "Be unobservant here, good friend, be free / Of the sharp moments when the shadow sly / Grows plain at his cold work."[21] "But At Last," the final Joy poem, and one well discussed by Thorpe, attempts to believe that "To slumber and to wither / Must be some difference," but finds that "Death's image at last" will break through even symbols "where quiet seemed immanent."[22]

Blunden's most constant attitude toward death was a kind of quiet defiance—the sort he learned in the war. In his most famous poem of all, "The Midnight Skaters," he urges "Earth's heedless sons and daughters" to defy the death that lies beneath the ice:

> Dance on this ball-floor thin and wan,
>   Use him as though you love him;
> Court him, elude him, reel and pass,
> And let him hate you through the glass.[23]

The kind of self-imposed illusion described in "Children Passing," realized for what it is, must sometimes be employed as a survival tactic, much as the "respite" of nature in the war had to be imposed even when its falseness seemed all too demonstrable. "Winter Stars" is almost a cosmographical inversion of "The Midnight Skaters": death comes at man not from below, but from the stars "ready to roar / Their sparkling death-way down. . . ." Men must fight the universe, and they sometimes, but only briefly, do well: "Watching each angry star / I thought our thicket lifted its stack of bayonets / Stiffly against the overthrow of Nature's parapets. . . ."[24]

Richard Church argues successfully that poems like "The Midnight Skaters" show a poet who "surely . . . is no bucolic escapist."[25] Death was indeed a constant part of Blunden's vision, a grim presence in his poems on the progress and origin of life itself. But he was able to see beyond it; he supported what he understood to be Coleridge's feeling that "if the human being simply stops at death, then we are just nonsense and the universe is meaningless."[26] Death itself does not provide the master key to this universe—or to a better one. As for suicide: "where even Hamlet attained no decision / It will be well to wait larger vision."[27]

Mutatis Mutandis

Church is also one of the few critics who have noticed the importance of time in Blunden's poetry: a "tragic sense of the mutability of things pervades his work, and it stains his phrases and images so emphatically, that no adverse critic could accuse his verse of being colourless, or lacking in a personal thumb-mark."[28] It was the war, as Church understood, which exacerbated what was probably a naturally hypersensitive time-consciousness in Blunden. The war that saw "Each moment puffed into a year with death,"[29] and dragged his postwar self continually back in time, sharpened this native awareness into pain. What Chloe asks herself about Duncan in *We'll Shift Our Ground* is a question Blunden had to ask himself: "What was this Time, that had crowded an inexhaustibly terrible drama into the brief dates of such as this enthusiast?"[30] In that same novel Blunden and Miss Norman put the serious issue of much of Blunden's philosophical verse in whimsical terms: "Those who have seen the recluse-like figure of Professor Einstein passing with the grace of the Romantic Movement over the speed-maddened street of a modern town will have felt, as from an object lesson, the fact that periods co-exist, that you cannot cut off time in blocks, that the expression 'one damn thing after another' is unscientific."[31]

Blunden's initial awareness of time was benign; it came through his youthful observance of the seasons. An understanding of time as a series of renewals was inculcated early and remained with him as a hedge against the darker view to which he later fell prey. Continuing harvests, he saw, give labor meaning and reward. The farmer brings home his "Gleaning," and "each good wife crowns weariness with pride, / With such small riches more than satisfied."[32] Time, in the field, reveals nature's inexhaustibility. The innocent love and festivity celebrated in "The May Day Garland" make the wish to rein time seem almost possible of fulfillment:

> The May should never fade to-night
> Could Time but be beguiled,
> Could Time but see the beauty of
> These singing honied hours,
> And lie in the sun adream while we
> Hid up his scythe in flowers![33]

Some crocuses at Trinity College show that "[s]ome of Time's own children are free of his own rule and scheme."[34] At "Weserland, 1939," there is proof that "good hours . . . / May just suffice if husbanded"; here time is just "shrewd old time," a benevolent figure who allows the creatures of the country "his plain dole."[35]

But far more often it is the savage effects of time that Blunden notes; the cyclical aspect of nature is time's sop, cruel and tantalizing. Time usually checks rather than enhances man's joy of nature: this is the theme of a number of poems in what is perhaps Blunden's darkest volume, *English Poems*, published in 1925, while he still mourned the death of Joy, was lonely in Japan, and was particularly troubled by war memories. In "The Shadow," the poet realizes that even in a sunny dell

> old time slyly all the while
> Checks the song and dims the smile,
> And sense so eager turns to shade,
> In silence stumbling through the glade.[36]

In "A Fading Phantom," "chilly [runs his] summer blood / To know Time's fluttering sign."[37] The poet wishes to be "untimed by the stern sun,"[38] but knows that his chief solace must be the realization of the even distribution of time's doom. One can attempt aphoristic comfort, answer rhetorical questions by conventional wisdom, but time will have its will; comfort must be sought in the knowledge that however horrible Joy's fate was, it is the universal one:

> The spider dates it not but spins in the heat,
> For what's time past? but present time is sweet.
> Aye, in that churchyard lies fruit of our loins—
> The child who bright as pearl shone into breath
> With the Egyptian's first-born shares coeval death.[39]

From Japan in this period Blunden confessed "murderous feelings towards time" to Edward Marsh.[40]

Those feelings never ceased to destroy moments of apparent serenity. In "I Just Noticed . . . ," the poet reflects on the demise of an old tower whose permanence had seemed assured:

> The signs were there, the mortal law
> Ran written on the gate;
> But not till sudden now I saw
> That savage "Out of Date."[41]

Blunden's pleas for preservation of the countryside were excited by impulses as much metaphysical as environmental. Time was an idea he apprehended not just as feeling, but as a living presence. The poem "A Connoisseur" is a remarkable exercise in extended personification: Time is seen as a magpie and a miser, not "a mere insensate mill of hours." He is a crazy acquisitor who never ceases to "swell the mad collection of his loves."[42]

Time's rapacity can be so subtle, however, that many of its effects go almost unnoticed; they are recognized after the fact. Time kills the "lyrical impulse" in such youths as "The Lost Leader"—a kind of working-class Chatterton of the army kitchen memorialized by Blunden in prose shortly after the war.[43] Age, experience, and practical affairs do their coarsening. So certain is time's victory that Blunden, a skillful practitioner of the sonnet and longer lyric in octosyllabic couplets, can rarely summon enough confidence to deliver even the *carpe diem* theme often expressed in those Renaissance forms. There was also, with respect to time, something eerie in his choice of subjects for his critical prose. They were uncommonly often poets who died young: Shelley, Keats, Chatterton, Kirke White. Death was almost seen as having been, for them, a paradoxical prophylactic against decay and aging. And if not death, then madness: the deliria of Smart, Cowper, and most importantly John Clare commanded his attention and sympathy. He was unusually sensitive to the vulnerable aspects of his more "normal" subjects, such as Lamb, as well. As Alec Hardie noted: "Nearly every author whom he examines has not only something of the purely poetic about him, a spark of visionary fire, but some personal reason for deserving sympathy as a man; prolonged ill-health, madness, suicide, or some inability to deal with the circumstances of his time."[44] These subjects were not so much the sentimental choices of a poet-critic often wrongly perceived as growing old untroubledly amidst academic insulation as they were spirits for whom Blunden had genuine empathy. His concern with time became, in his later years, more specifically a concern with his own aging. In *A Hong Kong House*, which shows the greatest Japanese influence in style of all Blunden's books, although still not as profound a one as one might expect, he tries to be optimistic in the face of decline, but is often forced to retreat into happy childhood memories in a new strategic movement against time. The poem "Once on a Hill" faces the fact that "nothing shall placate the will of time," but realizes nevertheless the simple mitigating wonder of recollection: "But a hill there was, and on that hill was I."[45] Even so, time reigns with little challenge; age and death cannot be dismissed even when the "Voice of Spring" is heard:

> while we wing, I see
> A snowfall from each pleasant tree;
>
> And none must see me weep,
> Or trace my footsteps towards my early sleep.[46]

When Blunden was in mid-career, Richard Church sent him a letter praising *An Elegy* and declaring that he heard in that collection "an increasing terseness, a 'dryness,' and soon, when you are even more venerable, we shall have to christen you Old Ironic. For that will be your general tone in the years to come."[47] There is only a small element of truth in this comment. One might regard some of the collections of the 1930s as more self-assured than the particularly dark work of *English Poems* from a decade before, and one might see a more quiet resignation still in *A Hong Kong House* in spots, but the constant shiftings of mood in the face of such forces as time, the inability to reach any final assurance, stand out more than any steady development of attitude or style. Blunden surely did not end his days as an ironist—particularly when it came to time. He strove, as he believed Shelley had, for an appreciation of its grandeur: "The Mutability of Spenser was a goddess 'all unworthy of the heaven's rule,' who was to be supplanted by steadfast Eternity. In Shelley's beautiful little poem ["Mutability"] she is herself Eternity." And yet he realized that "we find vicissitude" at last in that poem, too.[48] His own poems tried to search out some pleasure in a terrible truth. "An

Ancient Goddess: Two Pictures" attempts an even-handed dealing with
Time, first pessimistically, then otherwise. [49] There was "The Excellent
Irony" to note that it was after all Time who sent him love: "A voice, a
face, / A grace made all his hours one dance. "[50] He even tried to believe in
Julian Huxley's ideas of progress, although he had to remain skeptical:

> And Time himself learns,
> The undiscerning discerns,
> Time's progeny turns
> From old error, old discord, old malice, old fear,
> (Say the watchers) a little with every new year. [51]

Time, personified more than any other idea in Blunden's verse,
remains defiant and alive; it fights back in its own words in the light
poem "A Chronomachy: Or Let the Best Man Win":

> "That I am hated for being slow,
> When rapidity would be good,
>
> And for racing away when most desired
> To dally and defer;
> I let that pass. But am I tired?
> But am I tired? No, *Sir!*"[52]

Like any enemy of some duration, it becomes something of a friend. All
of Blunden's darker preoccupations call on him casually, constantly, and
the results are poems that show an odd familiarity between the poet and
his grave themes. "The Lawn," which deals with his young family in
Tokyo in the late 1940s, has an opening that indicates the ease of many
of Blunden's embarkations upon abstract journeys:

> The day was done: I mused alone,
> Asking for you, but not with moan,
> Since you, dear Wisdom, and I are grown
> Philosophers. But this runs on.
> To move us out, as boat, or theme:
> This evening, there was I alone,
> And calm the lawn lay in the gleam
> Of day's departure, and the moon. [53]

Amor Vincit Omnia

In the light love poem "An Aside," in *Halfway House* (1932), Blunden, attempting to show how aesthetic theorizing in the face of love is folly, minted an octosyllabic couplet worthy of the best of Herrick and Marvell: "About the stern defining phrase / A gay indefinition plays . . . ."[54] Love in his poetry is a powerful transformer of experience, a joy, a solace, and something whose gifts may be mangled by his own dark moods; it is, in short, more like nature for him than anything else. His ideas of it were shaped in much the same way as his other important feelings and beliefs: by having his early country experience disastrously modified by the Great War.

His youthful reading and acquaintance with natural surroundings prepared him to compose such early love monologues as "The Covert," spoken by a boy and filled with archaic diction and mythological reference. But Blunden's intelligence was always as critical as lyrical, and he could never long avoid the questioning personal voice. Even in "The Covert" the speaker shifts in the last stanza from being the boy to the poet himself, in a dying fall that attempts to put distance between the poet and the attitudes expressed just before with such lyric confidence:

> —Thus murmured to himself the boy
> Where all the spinneys ring
> With as rich syllables of joy
> As ever hailed the spring.[55]

This is an ominous distancing; the boy is made vulnerable by the dash which separates him from the wiser poet—a poet made mature in love, as in all else, by war wisdom; one who had to hold love in his heart when "lost in tortured days of France!"[56]

Just as the war made nature more desperately beautiful, and time more powerful in its swellings and shrinkings, it intensified Blunden's perceptions of love and friendship: "on shipboard, they say, people soon fall in love; in war, you fall in friendship, and know your neighbour as you probably will never do otherwise."[57] The intense affection of one soldier for another is strongly voiced by him in poems like "Battalion in Rest."[58] Time might always defeat "some cobwebbed boyish vow" of ordinary village friendship, but the ghosts of the war, each of whose survival depended on the other, are bound eternally.[59]

Blunden's celebrations of love are stylistically varied, showing the influence of his enthusiasm for different poets and literary periods.

There are the longer narrative poems such as "The Nun at Court" and "Thomasine": the first is in the sturdy manner of Browning, and the latter, from the Second World War, plants an expression of faith in love's ability to overcome the ugliness of the world and "the tangles of chance and time" in a story that has the exciting power of anticipation one finds in Keats's "Eve" poems.[60] There are also simpler lyrics like "Harbour Sketch: Written in Absence" which combine the signs of modern times—"The Guinness gospel on the wall"—with Renaissance rhythm and diction: "I want but One, so near, so far, / And have her cheek on mine by love."[61]

Most satisfying of all, and the best showcases for Blunden's talents, are his celebrations of homely, enduring country love, such as "Village Song" and "Lonely Love." The latter is an exquisite lyric which honors love among the plain and no longer young, and manages to remain unsentimental: this humble love sustains the poet as well as the lovers; they share with him "the strangest happiness."[62] The poem is a worthy companion piece to the earlier "Almswomen." Blunden is more self-assured in these poems about love's simple comforts than in such rare and mild attempts at eroticism as "To—":

> O rosy courage, soft resolve
> That pinioned thee so amorous fast, —
> Thither my passions now convolve
> And yearn to whelm thee so at last![63]

Blunden's primness and reticence have been exaggerated by his critics, but it is true that the passionate and erotic make up a territory not often or well explored in his verse.

He is predictably concerned with expressing the ties that bind love and the land. The poet in love will have a heightened sense of nature's beauty and power. This relationship is expressed in a number of poems, among them "Lovelight," "Fulfilment," and "Among All These," in *Shells by a Stream*, composed in the early 1940s when Blunden, despite and in defiance of the war, was in love with Claire Poynting, whom he married in 1945.[64] Love brings unity to the landscape riven by the war: "her young face / Charmed into one all else he knew. . . ."[65] In the same period, in *Cricket Country*, Blunden confessed: "Never was there a poorer naturalist than I, but I have loved Nature and am able to be as pleased with her characteristic looks and preoccupations and voices as with those (almost) of my true love."[66] He frequently addresses nature in his poetry as a lover might; here was an emotional phenomenon and technique he saw carried to extremes in the poetry of John Clare, whose thwarted love made "a great part of his verse . . . a history of the transference of love in him from woman to Nature."[67]

Love's pleasures are also much like the land's in their vulnerability. They can be given and taken away capriciously by the "south-west wind of the soul," and are dependent on one's relative freedom from the war and war memories. As late as his thirty-fifth birthday, "November 1, 1931," the war isolates Blunden from his friends and even his beloved: on the day that in biblical terms should mark the completion of half his life, he is unsure of both his past and his direction; he takes a walk, from his residence in Merton College, "[m]istaking Magdalen for the Menin Gate." He knows he is in the debt of his beloved for easing the pain of war memories, but tonight he will not seek her. He must apologize:

> from my silences your kindness grew,
> And I surrendered for the time to you,
> And still I hold you glorious and my own,
> I'd take your hands, your lips; but I'm alone.
> So I was forced elsewhere, and would accost
> For colloquy and guidance some kind ghost.[68]

But if love's solace is imperfect, and if, like nature, it is a sometimes illusory respite from horror, it must be sought and reverenced: one must impose upon oneself a belief in its healing power. It is most often this quality in his beloved which Blunden selects to hymn:

> Look, and all my prowlings clear;
> Speak, and desperation dies;
> Come my way, and fury flies;
> Joy, and man's huge chaos lies
> Calm in calm atmosphere.[69]

After love's early ardor dims, a "daily sustenance" remains; Blunden returns often to this quality usually neglected or sentimentalized in lyric poetry. He examines "A Not Unusual Case":

> I wonder when it happened, their last kiss;
> But maybe more than any kiss can give
> Dwells in their composition: smile who will,
> They thread the maze that baffles beauty still.[70]

When love is finest, it makes the former soldier's having "[d]odged many deaths" worthwhile;[71] in the Second World War it is able, sometimes, to make death count "for nothing, proved a lie,"[72] and give a poet a "sense of wide free ways, so free / And wide that I count nothing of time and space, / But think these present gifts will ever be. . . ."[73] On 20 February 1940, Blunden rejoiced in the love of the young woman who was later to become his wife; it is again the healing power of love, love as a hedge against destruction and time, that is singled out for commemoration in his diary, as it is in his most successful love poems: "Now today I have seen, what I might have done before without special vision, that there was a necessity behind this discovery of C. and all I feel for her. The war, one way driving me to despair in view of all I still retain dreadfully plain from the former war, forced an alternative: to find some home or abiding-place with the new generation who have never (so to say) been out of the shadow of war."[74] Five days later he completes the last page of this volume which "set out with the relapse of Europe into the bear-pit [on September 3, 1939]," still able to "honour a truth that will survive, and I dare assert, *Amor vincit omnia*, in 1940."[75]

He had to remain open to love's power, which was sometimes strong enough to let him defy time and darkness openly: "shatter me quite," he exclaims to them at the end of the sonnet "Millstream Memories."[76] His gratitude for such moments was such that he could often, in return, restrain himself from darkening those he loved any further with his own woes. Or even from imposing on them his particular joys: "Catherine Sings," a poem to his youngest daughter, ends with his generous refusal to impart his own nostalgia to a child born sixty years after her father:

> She was the winner; my fancy had failed,
> My lure was lost; and then
> I was glad that the new prevailed
> And the past comes not again;
> That little successor to me
> Claimed the future whatever it be,
> Its astonishing liberty.[77]

One must sometimes, in order to survive, force belief further than it can naturally go—this is the basis of many of Blunden's love poems. It is also the unifying idea among his many religious verses. In them most explicitly emerges the intellectual and emotional virtue he prizes above others—aspiration.

Deus et Homo

Blunden's religious poems can best be explored by beginning with the relationship he sees between God and nature: a relationship so close as to be a source of both happiness and jealousy for man. This closeness he felt had been perceived, albeit in different manners, by both Vaughan and Hardy, two of his favorite poets. They knew "that what we call nature might be more directly in touch with the Maker of all than man with his egotism and inverted powers has come to be."[78] It is to nature that Blunden goes to find evidence of God and to experience His power. Walking on a "young spring night," he hears

> a sigh unbosomed with such music
> That far and wide the forests and the farms
> Whisper, Arouse; 'tis God.
>   Having this love,
> Poor cheating Folly, should I wait on you?[79]

"'There is a Country'" where he, "an iota, atom, mote and grain, / May revel in this torrent God for hours."[80] In the volume titled *Retreat*, he expresses his openness to the rapture of night in lines that recall the mystical side of Vaughan that appealed to him:

> That far-sent patient messenger still
>   Woos him with sigh-soft hand,
> Appeals through endlessness until
> Response awakes with as deep a thrill
> As when dawn's gale of splendour shrill
> Storms with young force the general land.[81]

In these ecstatic moments the poet mingles with "shades that lived before Stonehenge stood."[82] There is in Blunden's moods of wildest nature appreciation a pantheistic element, a worship of "The Gods of the Earth Beneath." In that early poem from *The Waggoner*, the Traveller hears "the god of things that burrow and creep" tell of six gods of the earth who sense "one greater" God.[83] This sense of the presence of many gods is stronger in the most rustic poems of that first major collection of Blunden's verse than in later volumes, but it remained part of his theological and poetic makeup. In an essay on "The Unknown God" in the nature poetry of Vaughan, Wordsworth, Coleridge, and Shelley, he regrets the part of the English mind which sometimes represses the pantheistic impulse: "The miracle of Easter has its evidences in every meadow at that bright day, but these seem to be regarded as scenery, worth general reference perhaps, but not in the same spirit of sublimer reassurance as is proper within the four walls of our Church."[84] And in a verse address "To the Memory of Coleridge," he sees evidence that "pagan and Christian move / For the soul's health, and as in your wide world unite."[85] Once taken into account, however, it would be unwise to exaggerate this element in Blunden's religious thought and work, for he remained primarily interested in the "greater" God, the "Sun of Suns." Nature was first and foremost good *evidence* of a supreme existence. The geese in "Omen" make a "god-disclosing flight,"[86] and a "Summer Rainstorm" cleanses this divine evidence into comforting clarity:

> Joy's masque and fashion of Time's Samson-passion
> Deceives no lark that springs from weed and clod.
> Through their frank sight
> I feel the bright
> Angel-event of sunset's fresh creation
> And fields made lovely with the living God.[87]

God does not really emanate from nature so much as shine downward on it, animating its individual elements. But the location of God's presence shifted in Blunden's perception according to mood and purpose, and he would have regarded doctrinal neatness in this to be an expensive waste of his particular emotions and intellect. An emotional perception of God, in or above nature, was the highest goal of his religious experience.

The local tradition of religious observance he grew up in was simple and firm. Following church ritual was as much a part of life in Yalding as obeying the laws of the seasons: "Easter was no ideal ceremony but the bright triumph of spring; Advent was in every way the remedy, the hope of those dark and shorn weeks when life was drooping."[88] As a child he experienced easy familiarity with God: in the sketch "Bells on the Breeze," he tells how he and his young friends bargained with the Deity for some runs at cricket, or a roach or a chub on the ends of their fishing lines: "If Heaven granted the boon, we undertook not to break into the plantation on the way home; if not, we were free, and willing, to take our cherries or apples. I am not sure whether even this was the final state of that theory of prayer."[89] If not quite noble, here surely was a simple and direct relationship with God! And that is the kind of arrangement Blunden most admired. In "Hardham," in the early *Pastorals*, he shows his preference for rustic low-church ritual as a more direct link with God than any more elaborate worship would be:

> The smallest things are made divine,
> The low old pews, the narrow tiles
> Deep red, that pave the tiny aisles,
> The books whose gildings no more shine.
> O hamlet church, O mightly shrine.[90]

As for the "Mole Catcher": "What his old vicar says, is his belief," and Blunden envies his simple, unshakable, if unenthusiastic, faith.[91] And if you "Ask Old Japhet" he will tell you that the gospel truth is a " 'a jewel nobody touched, not yet' "—faith is too important to be left to the theologians.[92] Even the country parson, in "A Shadow by the Barn," draws back from religious argument: "'But from this brink of dangerous speculation / Let me recoil.'"[93]

Many of these poems of simple faith are monologues delivered by characters possessed of country diction and rhythm. Blunden does not sentimentalize or satirize these figures; he envies them their direct expressions of faith in the face of the twentieth century. They say what the poet sometimes cannot bring himself to say in his own voice. God Himself is sometimes imagined as a man of the country; the designer of a country church reckons that He needs

> Something between a castle and a cave,
> Indeed an immense byre and barn therewith,
> For that earth-lord to pace
> And thence watch out afield

> Triumphant in his seasons and their stride.

This God is a powerful squire, "Master of the endless world / Of clod, claw, root and man."[94] The English church meant community to Blunden, and the common aspiration of a congregation was often, in his poetry, taken as being itself evidence of the existence of a God and a heaven. Recalling the First World War almost fifty years after its close, in "Armistice: A March," he writes: "So many spires can hardly point in vain. . . ."[95]

Blunden's beliefs and doubts are emotional and often not particularly modern ones. His common sense tells him there is a heaven; it also tells him that this knowledge is sometimes precious little comfort to the men below it. The last stanza of the plainly styled "In Memoriam, A. R.-I.: Yokohama, November 1938," reads:

> I for one am prone to take
> The fact of death as far from final;

> Would one's Maker stoop to break
> The course of hope and undesign all?
> Still I have this present case,
> Another man I prized is dead. . . .[96]

The nature of God forces one to reconcile His good and evil; this is the central issue of several poems. The more forlorn parts of a village present "The Puzzle":

> The dead leaf on the highlands,
> The old tramp on the mill drove,
> Each whirls on nor understands
> God's freezing love.[97]

The natural world offers abundant examples of the troubling coexistence of Blake's tiger and lamb. It is easy to know that the "young moon" comes "from some calm triunion's brow," but what of the storms that follow?[98]

More often than not the opposing elements resolve themselves into an endurable whole. In *Near and Far* (1929) the poet gives his "Report on Experience," acknowledging that it was "peculiar grace" to live to see the war's devastation and then the destruction of what he thought had been a perfect love. But:

> Say what you will, our God sees how they run.
> These disillusions are His curious proving
> That He loves humanity and will go on loving;
> Over there are faith, life, virtue in the sun.[99]

God remains, like love and nature, another source of solace. The poet's direct, Donne-like addresses to Him in verse are rare, but he sometimes calls on Him, "[u]nasking what Thy form or mind may be," to sustain his faith in the face of sorrow.[100]

Blunden's poetry does not inquire deeply into the exact form of God or the origins of the universe. Like old Japhet he is largely untroubled by such questions. He can leave the debate over the godly or accidental origins of a "Running Stream" to "sage, saint, seer. . . ." The streams have never "revealed if a spirit indwelt their bubbling adown."[101] He enjoys these questions of origin; they do not bedevil him. They provide him with musings, and, in this case, merely add to the pleasure he takes in the stream. Poems such as "The Deist" and "The Atheist," both from

Poems 1930—1940, are less concerned with the intellectual validity of the professions of such believers and nonbelievers than with narrative projections of the dramatic and legal conflicts they generate.[102] Commentators have wondered whether Blunden's religious poetry is insufficiently rigorous in a post-Darwinian world. Michael Thorpe, for example, writes: "In Blunden, as in another loosely labelled 'Georgian,' Edward Thomas, there is a tension between the old Romantic 'cosmic consciousness'—sometimes really felt but often only willed or desired—and the disenchanted, modern mind. They are both nature poets of mood and occasion, their attitudes and hopes unsettled."[103] Hoxie Neale Fairchild views this situation more harshly, seeing in much Georgian religious verse "the sentimental naturalism of the eighteenth-century preromantics, in which the deistic religion of nature has not yet become fully pantheized." These same poets' awareness of modern science, he argues, makes them too "timid" to express more than "a thin and spurious theism";[104] as for Blunden, he places him in a group of poets who "think of religion more regretfully than mockingly."[105] Despite the justice of some of his observations where the Georgians in general are concerned, Fairchild is a troublesome commentator, not only because he is nastily suspicious of so many poets' sincerity, but because he confines his illustrations, in Blunden's case, to quite unrepresentative poems. What Thorpe would call "tension," Fairchild calls timidity, seeming to insist that poetry be either wholly rational or theistic. Blunden's undoctrinal religious verse annoys him.

It might surprise Fairchild and others that Blunden was more comfortable with Hardy's theological scheme than many other poets'. The poet whose deterministic verses made Chesterton call him the "village atheist" was still, Blunden chose to remind us, "no exotic, no outlaw, though his intellectual imagination could set him apart."[106] Blunden quoted Brig.-Gen. J. H. Morgan's recollections of a conversation he had with Hardy in October 1922: "'"I believe in going to church [said Hardy]. It is a moral drill, and people must have something. If there is no church in a country village, there is nothing. . . ."'"[107] Blunden of course realized the extent to which Hardy was troubled over the nature of the "First Great Cause," but he did not want Hardy's readers to ignore "an element of melioration, of submission and goodwill which is too easily forgotten in discussion of his creed."[108] This religious longing in Hardy, visible in poems like "The Oxen," helped him withhold, in his last years, according to Blunden, "the utterance which, he said, could only add to the burden of those whom he could inform of something like universal tragedy."[109]

This longing Blunden understood and admired. He himself was not unaware of the scientific revelations of his own century and the one before, but he chose optimism and aspiration, reminding us that Darwin himself felt his science would "open new and unsuspected regions of truth for man's discovery and thus, in the end, . . . make man's consciousness and sense of the rights of nature more distinct, more alert."[110] Having experienced the "Death of Childhood Beliefs"[111] with the arrival of the Great War, Blunden nevertheless came home from the front to deplore the modern soul's insistence that it is "[e]nough for us to lantern our own night."[112] On a "Stormy Night" he wishes to hear the bells of the faithful ring; the particular discoveries and horrors of the twentieth century are no excuse for a silence into which earlier troubled centuries did not retreat:

> How once these bells proclaimed the spirit of man,
> When, though in kennelled alleys the lean forms
> Of incurable disease and twisted mind
> Multiplied, still that music topped the wind,
> And aspiration soared in clanging storms
> To prove the triumph of a desperate plan.[113]

The church spire "ever declares that man's desire / Is godly, gracious. . . ."[114]

Blunden admired seriousness in religious matters, even if the conclusions a man was led to were not his own. Gibbon's *Decline and Fall of the Roman Empire*, with its flaying of Christianity, was still, to Blunden, "the greatest book, all in one, that an Englishman has written."[115] He treated Shelley's *Necessity of Atheism* with respect, and endorsed Dowden's recognition of its logic.[116] He rejoiced in the comfort Sassoon's conversion to Catholicism brought that friend: "you have chosen. I am glad."[117] He rebuked Joseph Severn's biographer for sneering at the attempts of James Augustus Hessey to console Keats, in his final illness, with religion: "Hessey belonged to an age when there was nothing strange or absurd in drawing the thoughts of the dying towards some larger consolation; and Keats himself turned in his extremity to the devotional manual of Jeremy Taylor."[118] Lamb "honoured all sincere forms of worship, and the attitude of devotion and of aspiration wherever found."[119] The longer Blunden himself lived the more fervently he wished to see an ecumenism of spirit:

> The time comes round when all the faiths and fears
> With which I marched or trembled

> Should in the audit of so many years
> Be in one truth assembled. . . .[120]

There was in this man of what so often appears a calm devotion a mystical streak as well—one he appreciated in his literary subjects. He preferred Vaughan's spiritual leaps to Herbert's methodical journey; he would rather wait for sudden religious experience in an attitude of receptivity than seek it through structured meditational exercise. "The Correlation,"[121] from the 1920s, and "Chimes at Midnight," three decades later, both describe his amazement and gratitude when visited by rushes of faith. The latter concludes:

> Now may I sing with something young
> Reborn in answer to your choir,
> And let that seraph touch my tongue
> With such divine desire
> As passed just now through this slow frame,
> And uttered all in one great Name.[122]

It was this easy, occasional quality of spiritual movement that T. S. Eliot objected to in Blunden as early as 1927. In a review of Blunden's book on Vaughan, Eliot decried Blunden's preference for that poet over Herbert: "Mr. Blunden, like some persons of vague thinking and mild feeling, yearns towards a swooning ecstasy of pantheistic confusion."[123]

Blunden would reply that the poet should let the spirit move him whenever it will. He regretted that the "religious unrest of Wordsworth and of Coleridge, though neither man ever ceased to have moments of vision scarcely in agreement with his formal theology, was reduced into an acceptance of Christianity, the Trinity, and the Church of England."[124] Blunden might himself accept these things, but with less intellectual sacrifice. His reason told him that in all matters of the mind "flashes" were more reliable than systems.

At the end of his address on "Religion and the Romantics," Blunden appended representative textual selections for a Japanese audience. One was "A Defence of Elia Against the Charge of Want of Religious Feeling," in which Lamb wrote: "The shapings of our heavens are the modifications of our constitution; and Mr. Feeble Mind, or Mr. Great Heart, is born in every one of us."[125] Blunden's religious poetry springs from the temporary dominance of any one of these temperamental qualities inside himself; in that poetry he shows the same persistent shiftings that mark his poems on other ideas. In "From the Flying-Boat" he may wonder of God: "Why hides He His face?"[126] But at other times his heart will be greater; "Cathedrals" are the real "starships,"[127] and man has only to allow his spirit to be moved by forces not from within:

> It is but yours to chime and dawn, not trace:
> For there are gleams of sun and gleams of God,
> And bells in heaven, prime campanology—
> Hear, and be sphered above; nor pry nor prod. . . .[128]

He was a man at peace with both his born institutional affiliation and new religious influences. He playfully wrote Edward Marsh from Japan in 1925: "In spite of the lotus I remain C. of E., and don't go to church."[129] He was a doctrinally casual poet, and this has proved infuriating enough to men like Eliot and Fairchild. But the simplicity of his poems of aspiration, in the face of his century and his own grim experience, gives him, in the eyes of others, an assured place in the modern writing of religious poetry.

"Experience and Record"

Blunden always held the Arnoldian view that poetry should be a "criticism of life" in the largest sense, and he was troubled more by the increasingly political nature of the poetry of the mid-twentieth century than by any formal innovations. One of the phenomena he found attractive in the Romantic age he chose to study was that "a man's opinion on futurity and salvation were then as momentous, among those who knew or read him, as nowadays is his attitude to political systems."[130] Life itself, he felt, should be poetry's province; guesses, unsystematic ones, should be made at its meaning.

For that meaning he went first to the land, for its appearance, with all its changes and constancies, could be equated with the movement of a human life:

> "Do you remember," years away I hear,
> "One evening when we stood on Furzes Hill?
> Where have such evenings gone?" "I wish I knew."
>
> I well remember. It was dark, and clear;
> Happy, and sad, remote and near; stood still
> And glided by." "That's Life; I meant, the view."[131]

The natural world, he felt, was the best-equipped philosophical laboratory; those poets who knew it well had the most to tell us of life. Even Mao Tse-tung was "actually that old-fashioned type a nature poet, and even when on the march and leading his army he is fascinated by all natural circumstance, which he has imagery enough to unite with his Godwinian and Confucian design."[132] The English countryside, with all its variation, was for Blunden the richest in meaning of all. Scholars like John P. Mills are correct to note that Japan had less of an impact on Blunden's view of life than one might expect, and the reason for this lies probably in the way the Japanese landscape struck him.[133] In *A Wanderer in Japan* (1950) he conjectured "that the enchantment of Japanese scenery had been a reason for the comparative dearth of a clear philosophy and natural history in the annals of the country, at least until the modernisation and the excitation of untried abilities. The charm was too great. Why should men pursue something which would never be so beautiful and complete as the picture?"[134]

Despite his attraction to philosophical verse, Blunden was uncomfortable about placing a final interpretive stamp upon any phenomenon, and he was reluctant to have any experience overwhelmed by analysis. In his diary, on 18 November 1939, he wrote sympathetically of his second wife, Sylva Norman: "With Sylva one encounters the artist—the experience nine times out of ten is scarcely complete before the interpretive passion is tapping away. A tragedy."[135] In "A Change," he wrote:

> How lovely it was, when all that came my way
> Came an experience; when the strong weak world
> Just came my way.
>
> —Now there must be, behind these contrary forms,
> Dominant idea; purpose and planned theme.
> Who wrote that play?[136]

Even the final lines of a poem called "The Sum of All," which follows "A Change" and closes *Poems 1930—1940*, express a unity that is more a mood than something final.[137]

In the poems of *A Hong Kong House*, his last major collection, he continued to search for "A Life's Unity,"[138] indirectly expressing the wish that his own final utterances would be full of the "Mercy and peace met together"[139] that he found in Shakespeare's last plays. But in "Summer Storm in Japanese Hills" he recognized the insoluble difficulty of knowing anything for certain in "the wan-hued tempest world / Where rock and tree like spindrift hurled / Will know as much as we at last."[140] And yet it was still the function of poetry to try to "peep" beyond. As far back as 1932, in his Clark lectures on Lamb, he had worried about the replacement of a dreaming "romantic man" with a controlled, statistical one.[141]

The poet should be a thinker and a dreamer, but he must not force his instants of revelation into ordered philosophy: "Mastery in poetry consists largely in the instinct for not ruining or smothering or tinkering with moments of vision."[142] The immediacy of the idea should be preserved even as the poem is, as it must be, shaped.

In his address "Experience and Record," Blunden said: "We cannot hope to bring all experience into the same diagram. This ocean of life is too vast to be represented in one kind of blue, grey, green or golden."[143] Blunden's poetic corpus is appropriately multi-colored, but it does not constitute a case of trying to "have" things both or many ways. What a critic like Fairchild perceives as a lack of rigor might more properly be called, in Blunden, lyric sincerity. This brings one back to the nature of his war writings: there too he was unable and unwilling to erect the coherent intellectual scaffolding that might support epic treatment of that experience at the expense of accuracy in portraying the vagaries of a half-century of feelings. Nearing his seventieth year, Blunden was lucid in his refusal to express more than guarded optimism—but unafraid to express that much: "The world seems, on the face of it, so darkened with crime and idiocy at the moment that the other faction, the angels, are working hard too, and I think in the end they will probably get ahead."[144]

Chapter Six

A Quiet Place: Blunden and Twentieth-Century Writing

A Poet Apart

If Blunden's poetry is best summed up as being meticulous and sincere, there will still be the objections of critics like David Daiches, who claims that Blunden's

verse lacks vitality; it solves no problems, achieves none of that quick cutting to the heart of things which some of his younger contemporaries, using a more difficult and a more complex dialectic, have on occasions managed. The meditations of a sensitive yet in some respects an academic mind, his work does not achieve the vision which shifting values and a worn-out medium demanded, and as a result most of his poems lack that burning core and complete integration which we find in the poetry of those poets who, wresting language to meet the urgency of their own problems, by being "modern" produce what will nevertheless have meaning and vitality for future generations.[1]

This is a basically fair-minded expression of the disapproval Blunden's poetry sometimes meets, and it must be taken into account in an attempt to evaluate his place in twentieth-century poetry. Blunden, while alive, was almost always regarded as a skillful poet well worth reading, but he was a poet apart. He and his traditionalist allies, such as Siegfried Sassoon and Richard Church, perceived themselves in this way. They knew they were not traveling the main poetic route of their times. Blunden's own reaction to the mainstream was a mixture of confusion, amusement, and occasional bitterness, and an examination of his own work, as well as the work of the "moderns" themselves, helps illumine his place in the world of poetry from 1920 to the present, and aids one in attempting to evaluate the fairness of a critical verdict that has been largely constant for several decades. Preliminary to even this examination, a brief look at Blunden's own standards and practice of criticism will be helpful.

The Heir to Elia

Blunden's critical essays, literary biographies, and reviews could in themselves be the subject of a useful book. But even a brief survey of that large and very rich body of work yields definite impressions of his perception of the critic's role. If ever a man came to praise and not to bury, it was he. His first major collection of essays contained *Votive Tablets*, studies that were *Chiefly Appreciative of English Authors and Books*. He saw no reason why criticism could not be what it had been in Sir Philip Sidney's hands—"shrewd and attractive, both at once. It is so often only one or the other."[2] The familiar style of the Romantic essayists he knew so well appealed to him in particular as a model for the critic in any age. In his book on *Keats's Publisher*, John Taylor, he quoted that man's definition of criticism with admiration and assurance: " 'I hate Criticism at all Times except when it is of that enlarged Kind that takes entire Surveys of a Subject, and conceiving old Writers to be new and new ones to be old awards to each his proper Share of Commendation. Besides in Poetry, I think Praise should be given where it is due, and that Silence is sufficient Dispraise.' "[3] It was the hostile reception of Keats's work that prompted this call for gentleness by Taylor in a letter to John Clare. It was a similarly generous spirit Blunden admired in Leigh Hunt's *Examiner*—the kind of temper which has often made modern critics of Hunt uncomfortable: "If [Hunt] preferred as he grew older to descant on the excellences and the happy evolution of humanity, is that a reason for treating him as so many idlers in literature treat him—like a shallow hedonist, a pious fraud?"[4]

Of the qualities of Blunden's own criticism, one might say what he said of the Duke of Cambridge, the late-nineteenth-century president of Christ's Hospital, concerning that man's battles with the reformers: "He loved; they dissected."[5] If his criticism is sometimes deliberately more "attractive" than "shrewd," it nevertheless performs the most important critical function of all—it charms the reader back to the text itself.

Blunden's greatest critical success lay in his practice of biography. In his books on Hunt, Lamb, and Shelley, one finds old-fashioned and comfortable portraiture. Attractiveness may again outweigh shrewdness, but these books are full of fresh readings, a poet's readings, and their scholarship, which is considerable, is artfully carried. There is always a posture, and it is always a celebrating one. Blunden never conceals his sympathies toward particular men and particular styles, and his own origins, personality, and work in poetry afforded him a unique view of his subjects. Despite their mutual attachment to the land and their acquaintance in the 1920s, some would be hard put to imagine a less suitable biographer for Thomas Hardy than Edmund Blunden. And yet Blunden, by relying on his own instincts and sympathies, managed to illuminate the more traditional and cheerful sides of Hardy better than many more "modern" sensibilities and pens have done. In his biographies, Blunden talks quietly to his readers. He thinks out loud, with deceptive casualness, about his subjects' personalities. He is fascinated by old-fashioned clues to character—particularly physiognomy. Always delighted by the discovery of new portraits, busts, and masks of his subjects, he puts them to use to understand the characters of Hunt, Hardy's parents, and more than one generation of the Shelley family.[6] Such conjectures serve to ease the reader into the "story," and stories are exactly what these books are. The lives of his subjects were for him as important as the works they produced. In his book on Hardy, he goes so far as to give us the story of Hardy's career separately, only afterwards taking up the task of explicating and evaluating the novels and poems.

The sympathy a biographer feels for his subject must be unashamedly expressed; and it should elicit a corresponding feeling in the reader. Blunden, as a reader, experienced an emotional reaction to Walter Peck's judicious but impassioned condemnation of Shelley for the suicide of his wife, Harriet, and he recorded it in a review that revealed his insistence on thorough scholarship and emotional involvement for any biographer.[7] His own involvement with his subjects shows up continually in his responses to their glories and difficulties; when the Hunt brothers quarrel, for instance, Blunden is noticeably distressed and saddened, a hundred years after the fact.[8]

One does not communicate such feeling through a scientific, detached style. One tells instead a story, and uses a nineteenth-century novelist's human, common sense, not a psychologist's labels, to comment on the action. A biography remains a tale. Blunden admits that his work on Hunt is a "book of rainbows and shadows," and for all his admiration of Walter Peck he must reprimand him for those moments when he is in danger of "losing the biographer in the critical technician."[9] The Freudian approach did not please or suit Blunden; Swift's personality might be "strange enough, but not so strange as some of the books which have been written about him in our age of psychological revelations."[10] Any writer, even two centuries after his death, is entitled to his privacy. This attitude may limit Blunden's own probings, and in such efforts as his introduction to Tennyson's poems it clearly does, but it does prevent him from wandering down certain blind alleys.[11] He did not avoid unpleasantness and real pain; quite the contrary, considering his choice of so many troubled subjects. But he felt it was the business of criticism to offer healing, rather than X rays, to such cases. Above all, it was the business of criticism to resurrect the lost. Blunden would have admitted that his fondness for "discoveries," from his earliest days, led him to a certain exaggeration in the advocacy of his "finds"; he once told how his classical master one day returned one of his schoolboy essays with the comments, " 'Try to keep a sense of proportion. One Robert Browning is worth twenty Lord de Tableys.' "[12] But, more importantly, the man who helped to edit three volumes of "Wayside" poems could "safely say after about thirty-five years of hunting for overlooked poetry in England, the supply seems practically inexhaustible."[13] In an essay on "The Country Tradition," Blunden protested that some subjects were overworked and that many minor writers "lack their curator."[14] Critical light should be distributed more evenly if criticism is to do its job. Blunden generously stops his narrative in *Leigh Hunt* to offer, in a footnote, Hunt's neglected Christmas writings to any young scholar in search of a thesis topic.[15]

Blunden gently and indefatigably explained and popularized English literature in the course of his diplomatic work in Japan and during his professorships there and in Hong Kong. He was an evangelist for the writers he loved best, and he took advantage of any opportunity to speak their names. A lecture on Sidney's sonnets given one evening at Hosei University in the late 1940s, for instance, gave him the chance to mention Lamb's estimation of those poems; so he took it, with obvious relish.[16] Indeed, Lamb is probably Blunden's closest critical cousin; the latter's combination of wisdom and affection toward his subjects, including Lamb himself, makes him a worthy heir to Elia. The same subjects and the same names occur again and again in his lectures and books, and are recited almost in the manner of a lover. The sense of intimacy and regard between subject and explicator is unusual and impressive.

A Particular Public

After his service in the war, and his brief career as a student at Queen's College, Oxford, Blunden began his public life as a writer to an enthusiastic response. *The Waggoner* (1920) and *The Shepherd* (1922) received warm reviews and attracted the notice of such important poets as Bridges and Hardy. As Sherard Vines, one of Blunden's fellow English writers in

Japan, remarked, translating political terms into poetic ones, these two volumes "were rightly hailed as an example of what the Right wing could still do despite the growing notoriety and eccentricity of the Left."[17] There was a danger in both the kind and degree of this enthusiasm, however. Blunden at once established an extremely high standard of work to live up to, as well as the sense of a particular Blunden "product." The "Right" claimed him, and thereby, to a certain extent at least, isolated him for the next half-century.

A. C. Ward has written that Blunden "was, perhaps, too good a poet at the beginning. If *The Waggoner* had appeared in 1930 instead of 1920, and had followed a series of inferior volumes, his admirers might have been more content."[18] Success may also have encouraged Blunden to be more prolific than was wise for sustaining his reputation. On 5 February 1923, Sir Edmund Gosse wrote him the following warning: "Do let me entreat you to take the trouble to polish your work. It is a danger for you that at your very early age you have met with nothing but praise. It is a very serious danger, because you are tempted, by the inconsiderate eulogy of a horde of silly critics to think anything you write excellent. I venture to say this, because I believe your natural powers exceed those of any other young man of your generation, and because it will be a keen disappointment to me if you allow yourself to be fooled into indolence."[19]

Michael Thorpe, one of Blunden's recent commentators, has speculated: "Had he revised more and published less, and laboured to load every rift with ore, many would estimate him more highly than they do—he would also, perhaps, have lost some devotees."[20] In order to gain more praise from the critical establishment that existed in his middle and later years, he would have risked alienating the readership he had, one which was eager for more of the same reliable and non-"modern" collections of verse. Blunden was himself well aware of this, but he defended his large output in the preface to *English Poems* (1925) as a poetical necessity, not just a popular one: "If half-ideas, verges of shadows and misty brightness . . . find their way into my story, I must often acquiesce, because I know by experience how such visitants come and go. . . ."[21] They were best captured alive.

Blunden inevitably failed to maintain the initial pitch of enthusiasm his early work and *Undertones of War* aroused in the critics. This was in part due to the natures of criticism and fashion, but also to the fact that the distance between Blunden and the main line of the century's verse was, by the 1930s, growing ever wider. Richard Church, who viewed himself as a partisan of Blunden's in a fight against modernism, stated the case, in a book published in 1941, with alarm—and exaggeration:

"After [*Undertones*], [Blunden] retired into the monastery of Merton College, and has since been heard of only in the cruel headnotes of the young derisionists. They have sneered at his 'nature' poetry, as they call it; and they have said more sinister things about reactionary political tendencies in the author of it. I have not heard a word of praise amongst them. I have not met a single disciple."[22] There was more than one word of praise, more than one disciple, and a great deal more respect than derision from the modern party, but it is true that by the 1930s Blunden had lost any chance to occupy the main stage. F. R. Leavis, in his terrifying way, pronounced his verdict, and it held. He found Blunden "significant enough to show up the crowd of Georgian pastoralists," but decided that in the later work the "visionary gleam, the vanished glory, the transcendental suggestion remain too often vague, the rhythms stumble, and the characteristic packed effects are apt to degenerate into cluttered obscurity."[23] Blunden was marked forever by others as either a mere traditionalist or an anachronism. But Blunden, to his credit, never made his dispute with the moderns into a cantankerous public one.

As perceptive a critic as Cyril Connolly confessed that, for all his admiration of Blunden's personality and feeling for the English and Japanese countryside, he had become so used to the modern poetic consciousness and style that Blunden's was not the sort of verse to which he could respond with sensitivity or even patience.[24] Blunden was more a figure of the past than the present—even sometimes to his closest friends and allies. In 1928 Sassoon wrote him: "I am so fond of your poetry that when I read it I sometimes find it difficult to believe that you are alive."[25] This may tell us more about Sassoon than Blunden, but it does give us a clue to part of Blunden's appeal to the majority of his readers.

Blunden was distressed about the turns poetry took after the First World War. He especially disliked its new political and "psychological" directions. The left-leaning poems of the Auden circle in the 1930s bothered him, as did, more generally, the tendency he perceived in modernism "to strive for effects in prose or verse by inventing the most vociferous agglomerations of terms that we can, and in the greatest possible number. Do we lose sight of style?"[26] He was certain that modern developments had narrowed rather than expanded poetry's province and appeal, and he was confused by other poets' inability to find the older forms and styles any longer usable. In *The Burden of the Past and the English Poet*, Walter Jackson Bate has written affectingly of the reasons for the modern revolt: "The drama of the historical development of twentieth-century poetry must be viewed in the light of its own uneasiness about its inheritance of the romantic lyric—with many of the

premises still shared and certainly with the same premium on condensa-
tion, but with the conviction that this particular resolution cannot again
be repeated for the simple reason that we now have this too behind us as a
further addition to our own, still heavier 'burden of the past,' a burden
that can truthfully be said to exist only in the imagination but is
nonetheless present."[27] Nothing could better highlight Blunden's separation from his own present than his unconsciousness of any such
burden. In that unconsciousness lay both his distinction and his limitations.

He felt that time would rectify the overly credulous reception the
moderns had received. He wrote Sassoon in 1937 of his belief that "we
shall see general criticism return to a better candour, and a new Oxford
book supplant W. B. Y[eats]'s incoherent item."[28] One man who would
be more amply represented in that anthology, according to Blunden,
was Sassoon himself. In 1953, he wrote H.M. Tomlinson that he had
recently been "involved in a discussion at Singapore when I ventured to
say that S. Sassoon was quite as important a poet as E. Pound. It all goes
back to the question What Is Poetry? & I suspect the Pounders don't
waste time on that."[29] Twenty-five years before this, in an essay on
Sassoon's poetry, he had given one of the key elements of the answer to
the question "the Pounders" do not waste time on: Sassoon's poetry "is
as *readable* as it is copious. . . ."[30] This readability, he felt with some
pain, was not so banal or anachronistic as the moderns felt. Poetry had to
be accessible to a wide audience. But poets who continued to be
"readable" were paradoxically doomed to obscurity by critical indiffer-
ence or hostility. In his manuscript of "Poetical Reminiscences," he
noted that the period of the early years after the First World War needed
an anthologist who would "leave the beaten track."[31]

Blunden and T. S. Eliot were acquainted—cordially. But Blunden
saw Eliot, in his role as high priest of modern poetry, as being in many
ways the bane of twentieth-century verse, and he expressed this feeling
in his letters to other equally aggrieved traditionalists. The perception
was, however, built on a foundation of friendliness and respect. In his
diary, on 8 November 1940, Blunden mentioned a pleasant visit from
Eliot, noting the latter's "gentlemanly simplicity" and hoping for the
chance to know him better. But three years later he would write Claire
Poynting that the Indian director of the BBC wanted him "to give 2
talks on the poetry of T. S. Eliot. I don't want to for the importance of
Eliot has already been wildly exaggerated."[32] This was the concerted
opinion of Blunden's conservative circle of writers, which included
Sassoon, J. C. Squire, Tomlinson, Church, and others. As early as 1925,

Tomlinson had written Blunden from Cardiff his reaction to a review in the *Nation*, by Leonard Woolf, which claimed that Eliot was the best modern poet. Blunden no doubt enjoyed Tomlinson's remarks:

Well, what is a poet? God knows. But if a poor soul lost in Limbo, like Eliot, who is chiefly aware "of the damp souls of housemaids" (which is not true, for many a kind little char has a warmer & more comfortable soul than the grey & saddened spiritual appendix of T. S. Eliot)—if, I say, he is a poet, then I am under the penalty of eating my tin hat. I've read this last volume of his—I've read, for conscience' sake Waste Land 3 times—& I felt as I do now in this dreary & drab Welsh hotel; perhaps he meant me to. Well, he pulled it off.[33]

If Eliot's defects could be put under two main headings, they would be his position during the First World War, and his doctrine of impersonality in poetry. Blunden could appreciate neither. Ian Donnelly records Blunden as having said in the mid-1930s: "'I don't know why Eliot should feel so badly about things. . . .There is no reason why he should have to write in that "I-cannot-be-gay" manner. He did not have to go through the war.'"[34] This is, of course, an unreasonable censure, but it is further evidence of the war's pervasive conditioning of Blunden's life and writings; more pertinently, perhaps, the introduction of the elusive persona of modern verse, so closely identified with Eliot, troubled Blunden and his faith in the Romantic lyric. In his biography of Hunt, Blunden had remarked that in the "patchwork of fineness and flippancy" that is *The Story of Rimini*, "one emerging merit is felt; there is personality here."[35] A modern author's self-imposed exile from his own verse was, to Blunden, a pointless pursuit of an "objectivity" that was unwanted in the first place. He would have agreed with J. C. Squire, who wrote him in 1930 that it was no poetic flaw to approach the English countryside in a personal way.[36]

Indeed, Squire was eager to have Blunden lead a movement against the modernists, who he felt were devoid of substance and style. As late as 1949 he was urging him to return from Asia "to join in the battle for sense and music here."[37] But Blunden never became loudly factional. One reason for his refusal to do so, besides his good sense and good nature, was his basic satisfaction with a reading public that belonged to him and the traditionalists in spite of everything else. For the most part content to do without fame and the label of "greatness," Blunden was willing to serve that constituency. Despite all obstacles, he and his kind continued to be read. He wrote Sassoon early in 1952: "Although we have been as you say put aside by the literary autocracy, I gather from a lecturing visit just done that general readers do not altogether ignore us. But they go mostly to the free libraries and there the selection is made by the new school of librarians, who must be in the fashion; and anthologies also both help & hinder their discoveries."[38] About a year before this Sassoon had written to Leonard Clark that "Modern poetry has brought its unpopularity on itself by disregarding much that cannot be disregarded with impunity. . . . "[39] This was the commonly held viewpoint of the "Right." Church wrote Blunden in 1964 that the two of them suffered "from literary fashion; the cult of violence, morbid self-consciousness, & the general denigration of a melodic line, the symbol of faith in the unity & pattern of divinity throughout the universe."[40] But even Church, with his intemperate views, knew that his and Blunden's "public remain faithful and also [that] it increases outside the small world of fashionable criticism and the academies."[41]

This loyal public was the one Blunden cultivated. He knew that they wanted "verse" as well as poetry—sometimes something with a lighter touch, free of anguish. In a note to *Choice or Chance* (1934), Blunden expressed hope that he would be forgiven for including "here a few pieces of lighter verse, which may at least indicate my admiration for the poets who can make jokes, and call Laughter a Muse."[42] In *Cricket Country*, he praised "the poetry of diversion" and pointed to examples of it in Milton, Shelley, and Coleridge, celebrating "that sovran humour which so freshens and endears our English poetry even when it most strenuously wrestles with the eternal perplexities. . . ."[43]

Writing the preface to his collected poems in June 1956, Blunden gave what amounted to a definition of poetry itself in a discussion of both the changes he saw in poetry in the twentieth century and his perception of his own audience. Despite the volatile pronouncements of professional critics, Blunden found the Common Reader "still very much on the scene," and felt himself still aware of the "principal thing": "poetry is as much a part of the universe as mathematics and physics. . . . The method of language for conveying some perception of the grace beyond the facts is open to all: for me the essence of the blessing is often given in some melody and sidelight by an 'unimportant' poet where I find the great ones marching on another objective after all."[44]

Blunden realized what place had been accorded him by the critics—a respected, minor one. He tended to be labeled as war poet or pastoralist or traditionalist, but he was never regarded as eccentric or anything less than skillful and genuine. As T. Earle Welby wrote: "there is such a thing as a continuously poetic susceptibility, a temper in which any moment might yield its poem. That susceptibility, that temper, are Mr.

Blunden's. He is a poet on several levels, and never the highest; but he is never other than a poet."[45] In a letter to Blunden in 1960, Sir John Betjeman called him the "most tender & least demonstrative & least ostentatious of our really Good poets."[46] Poets less "traditional" than Betjeman also admired Blunden's strength. Betjeman himself tells the following anecdote: "I remember Auden coming into my room [at Oxford] and appraising my shelves with the sure and precocious literary judgment he had even in his, [*sic*] teens. 'Ah! the usual stuff,' he said, 'but I see you have got *something* genuine.' And he picked out my volumes of Blunden, adding 'he's a good poet,' "[47] Blunden was mostly considered steady, dependable, and calm. But these qualities have sometimes been pointed to in ways that sentimentalize and diminish him. Hugh I'Anson Fausset makes a mistake in viewing Blunden as, "to a great extent . . . immune from the conflict which tests and torments so many of his contemporaries."[48] This sort of comment troubled Blunden himself. In his diary in 1941 he recorded his reaction to the reviews of his *Poems 1930–1940*: "The curious thing is that I should have a steady character in verse, being rather (I know) other than that in deed."[49] His more "modern" contemporaries did him both honor and a disservice in according him what Stephen Spender has called "a quiet place" in the poetry of the twentieth century.[50]

The climax of Blunden's critical reputation occurred with his election as Oxford Professor of Poetry in 1966. As early as 1938 he had been mentioned for the chair, but it was generally felt that he was then still too young. As H. W. Garrod wrote him: "I have agreed to go in with the [E. K.] Chambers crowd; and as I mentioned the matter to you long ago, I feel a duty to tell you. The truth is that EKC is old, and EB young (as we count years, here we grey-heads)."[51] In 1951 the post was again vacant, but Blunden withdrew in favor of C. Day Lewis, who generously responded: "it's another case of Gresham's Law, I fear—if that is the law by which the higher is driven out by the lower."[52] In a birthday poem for Blunden in 1946, Day Lewis had praised Blunden's natural modesty and quiet immunity to changes in literary fashion.[53]

But the poetical and critical establishments seem to have had a lingering sense of an injustice done to Blunden. In 1953, Garrod wrote him about assuming the Hong Kong post: "There's something the matter with this country, and with literature, when a way can't be found for keeping you with us. It's a disaster, and past understanding."[54] But by 1966 Blunden was home, and his turn for real public recognition had come. He was elected Professor of Poetry at last, securing 477 votes to 241 for Robert Lowell, for whom the undergraduate Poetry Society had campaigned. There was, however, a feeling among some that this was too much in the way of honor: "After Mr. Blunden won . . . the poet Stephen Spender called the loser " 'the most brilliant, original and serious poet of his generation' and suggested that undergraduates be allowed to vote in future. Older voters, it was said, had repelled the American 'invasion.' "[55] Some felt that this was an insufficiently "quiet" place for Blunden as he neared seventy.

But one poet who did not was Robert Lowell. Blunden had worried over the publicity the affair generated, and confessed to Lowell in a letter that his daily life had been "thrown . . . into disorder" by it.[56] Lowell offered congratulations and support: "I've admired your poetry for years, and rather felt as though and [sic] old friend were being set against me, when the controversy began to boil. I really should have withdrawn, when you were entered, but somehow didn't through inertia. The lectures too would have been a problem. Criticism comes slowly and imperfectly to me. Something might have come, but who knows? I hope you will find pleasure in the work you are bound to do with distinction. May cheerfulness set in immediately!"[57] I. A. Richards expressed pleasure that Oxford would enjoy Blunden's lectures, which he knew were as "natural as breathing. . . ."[58] Blunden held the post until 1968; ill health forced his resignation.

Blunden Country

In attempting to guide readers of today through the "Blunden country" that Walter de la Mare predicted more and more of them would discover,[59] one does well to keep in mind Alec Hardie's reflection that "anthologists have scarcely looked beyond a few of his early perfect pieces, deservedly popular but not adequate to represent his scope."[60] The thematic division of Blunden's works offered in this book suggests, it is hoped, that wider range which the anthologists should scan. Blunden was not a poet of simply one place, idea, or time, no matter what basic unity there may be in his voice and style. The poet of nature, the precisionist who brought forth such poems as "The Poor Man's Pig," becomes the poet of character, the splendid portrait painter of "The Shepherd" and the "Almswomen." And the recorder becomes a kind of visionary when he makes his rural locations the setting for such essentially philosophic works as "The Midnight Skaters" and "Winter Stars." No poet without Blunden's intimacy with the land could have produced war poems like "Rural Economy" and "The Prophet," but these works still do not prepare one for the poems of war memory, the inward psychological turnings of the haunted poems—his most outstanding contribution to the literature of the war. Any anthology which fails to consider examples of Blunden's work in all of these large areas dooms him to more of the critical pigeonholing he resented.

But one wonders if any anthologist can do Blunden justice, since no matter how fine any individual lyric is, including the ones just mentioned, he cannot be fully appreciated without reading him widely. Context is crucial to his work, because only when taken together do his poems give us a real sense of his personality and voice, any real sense of his having been, as he said, a man who "lived from one epoch into another."[61] As he said of Hunt's *Rimini*, "there is personality here. The composition is stamped with the author's image . . . a presence that is clearly recognisable. . . ."[62] Poetry indeed "must contain more"—and his does—but it is the personality and voice emerging from his work that will be prized most as time goes on. When one hears by itself a poem like "November 1, 1931"—"That war had ended my sublunar walk—/ Forgive me, dear, honoured and saintly friends; / Ingratitude suspect not; this transcends . . ."—one merely detects a voice.[63] Taken with his other poems of war-hauntedness, and those of other themes and subjects, one recognizes it and welcomes it, with all its apology, tentativeness, and care. The sense one gets of a personality troubled by its own century, although not in the usual way, gathers itself gradually, and the effect is ultimately substantial. The poems speak quietly, but there is a force in their accumulation that can be considered a legitimate part of their worth.

This must be one's answer to Daiches's objection that Blunden's verse "lacks vitality . . . achieves none of that quick cutting to the heart of things which some of his younger contemporaries . . . have on occasions managed." His poems do indeed cut more slowly and deliberately, and the entire body of work may lack the "burning core" Daiches finds in the single poems of the other poets. There is nevertheless, in the end, what Daiches calls an "integration." Blunden simply demands a certain patience and devotion, for the corpus is more important than any single lyric or theme. But Daiches's complaint is to a certain extent a legitimate one, in that the reader of modern poetry may be unwilling to invest so much in "personality" and expansiveness. The assertion of a critic like Fausset, however, that Blunden was relatively "immune from the conflict which tests and torments so many of his contemporaries," is potentially more harmful to the poet's reputation. But it can be combated much more easily than Daiches's objection. A reading of the smallest handful of Blunden's poems about death and time will disabuse any thoughtful reader of the idea of Blunden as a man removed from turmoil and, to use Aldous Huxley's phrase for Herbert's concern, "inner weather."

Blunden's reservations about modernism were serious ones, and perhaps sometimes ill-founded, but he did not retreat into silence or real rancor. It was inevitable and necessary that he maintain critical standards different from the currently prevailing ones if he was to be able to draw on his particular strengths in the practice of his art. He found the English tradition ample and catholic enough, and it was not dead or abused in his hands. He would have been oddly struck by the negative tone of the critical label "derivative," but he can be said to have replenished the tradition as well as taken from it.

He practiced his art with little material reward throughout a long career, and was remarkably free of self-pity. He was a genuine man of letters who served several different spheres of the literary universe—poetic, journalistic, and academic—with distinction. His diaries and letters would repay editing and publishing. A reader of those prose writings both published and unpublished will find himself regretting the books that might have been written but were not—the *Microcosmographie* recommended by Masefield, or perhaps a memoir of Oxford in the 1930s, a period of which he offers convincing glimmers in the diaries. The tutor of such notable poets as Paul Engle and Keith Douglas, Blunden continues to draw praise from his former students at Oxford, Tokyo, and Hong Kong. Taken together, his accomplishments in the face of war, periods of ill health, family difficulties, and a slender income are remarkable.

Criticism somehow fails Blunden in its utterance of the word "minor." That it will remain convenient to call him a minor poet is beyond disputing. But "minor" need not sound the dismissive note it usually does. Certainly that word was no obstacle to Blunden's own restoration and curatorship of so many neglected figures; no doubt he recognized ties between his own art and theirs. What he understood so well, and what his own commentators might better heed, is the very necessity of the presence in each English literary age of a quiet but distinct minor key. The seventeenth century heard Browne as well as Milton. Shenstone and Pope, Clare and Coleridge—they too produced the minor and major strains of their shared times. Eliot, Yeats, and Pound may give their names to our own age, but criticism will miscarry in its duty to "propagate the best" if it forgets that Edmund Blunden was here as well.

Notes and References

Manuscript materials marked "HRC" are quoted courtesy of The Humanities Research Center, The University of Texas at Austin. Materials marked "Berg" are quoted by permission of the Henry W. and Albert Berg Collection, The New York Public Library, Astor, Lenox and Tilden Foundations. Material marked "Houghton" is quoted by permission of the Houghton Library, Harvard University.

Chapter One

1. "Dead Letters (T. L. H.)," *English Poems* (London, 1925), p. 66.
2. "Criticism: Sidney to Arnold," *Addresses on General Subjects connected with English Literature* (Tokyo, 1962), p. 191.
3. Birth certificate of Edmund Blunden (HRC).
4. Alec Hardie, *Edmund Blunden* (London, 1958), pp. 5–6.
5. Letter from Edmund Blunden (grandfather) to Charles Edmund Blunden (father), 17 December 1895. Transcribed by Edmund Blunden (subject) in a book of ancestral and personal notes, documents and memorabilia (HRC).
6. Ancestral and personal notes, documents and memorabilia (HRC).
7. Ibid.
8. Ibid.
9. Ibid.
10. Untitled memoir of his father, autograph manuscript/unfinished (HRC).
11. Ancestral and personal notes, documents and memorabilia (HRC).
12. "An Empty Chair (Chas. E. B.)," *A Hong Kong House: Poems 1951–1961* (London, 1962), p. 61.
13. *The Face of England* (London, 1932), p. 58.
14. A. C. W. Edwards's contribution to *Edmund Blunden: Sixty-Five*, ed. Chau Wah Ching, Lo King Man, and Yung Kai Kin (Hong Kong, 1961), p. 87.
15. Hector Buck, "An Open Letter to Edmund Blunden," in *Edmund Blunden: Sixty-Five*, p. 51. Buck was a fellow student of Blunden's at Christ's Hospital.
16. "The Preamble," *Pastorals: A Book of Verses* (London, 1916), p. 11.
17. Untitled reminiscence of 1914, autograph manuscript, 28 August 1967 (HRC).
18. *Undertones of War* (New York, 1965), p. 23. (Originally published 1928.)
19. "A Summer's Fancy," *Halfway House: A Miscellany of New Poems* (London, 1932), p. 15.
20. Untitled reminiscence of 1914 (HRC).
21. *The Face of England*, p. 100.
22. Edward Marsh, Letter to Edmund Blunden, 8 October 1919 (HRC).
23. Letter to Edward Marsh, 15 October 1919. (Berg).

24. *Keats's Publisher: A Memoir of John Taylor (1781–1864)* (London, 1936), p. 105.

25. Blunden wrote an account of how he produced his celebrated "Almswomen" with Mary's aid. A typed carbon copy of it, two pages dated 25 April 1962, is in the Humanities Research Center collection.

26. For an account of this work, see Blunden's pamphlet *John Clare: Beginner's Luck* (Chatham: Bridge Books, 1971).

27. *Thomas Hardy* (London, 1951), p. 84. (Originally published 1942.)

28. "A First General Address," *Lectures in English Literature* (Tokyo, 1952), p. 13.

29. H. M. Tomlinson, Introduction to *The Bonadventure: A Random Journal of an Atlantic Holiday* by Edmund Blunden (New York, 1923), pp. 7–8.

30. Florence Hardy, Letter to Edmund Blunden, 17 January [1923] (HRC).

31. One version of the difficulties in the Blundens' marriage is given in the correspondence between Edmund Blunden and Lady Ottoline Morrell from 1921 to 1930, when Edmund and Mary Blunden were divorced.

32. "'How Should I Forget?'" *Japan Quarterly* 2 (1955):310.

33. "Looking Eastward," *An Elegy and other Poems* (London, 1937), p. 83.

34. Articles of Agreement between the Japanese Government represented by Mr. Takezo Okamoto, First Secretary of the Japanese Embassy, London . . . and Mr. Edmund Blunden of England . . . March 12, 1924 (HRC).

35. Yoshitaka Sakai, "Edmund Blunden, Teacher," *Today's Japan*, March-April 1960, p. 60.

36. "Unteachable," *English Poems*, p. 89.

37. "Winter Comes to Tokyo," *The Mind's Eye* (London, 1934), p. 102.

38. Sir Rupert Hart-Davis, *Edmund Blunden, 1896–1974, An Address by Rupert Hart-Davis, St. Bride's Church, Fleet Street, 7 March 1974* (Oxford, 1974), n. p.

39. Royal Society of Literature reports for 1969–70 and 1970–71, p. 59.

40. "November 1, 1931," *Halfway House*, p. 67.

41. Earl Miner, "Honor for Edmund Blunden," *Today's Japan*, March-April 1960, p. 44.

42. Letter to Sylva Norman, 9 May 1933 (HRC).

43. Diary, 28 September 1939 (HRC).

44. Laurence Brander, "Edmund Blunden, Book-Collector," *Today's Japan*, March-April 1960, p. 50.

45. Saito, "Edmund Blunden, Poet," p. 37.

46. Hardie, *Edmund Blunden*, p. 23.

47. Letter to Leonard Clark, 5 June 1953 (Berg).

48. Michael Thorpe, "To a Georgian Poet Found Pining in a Tropical Library," *By the Niger and Other Poems* (London: Fortune Press, 1969).

49. Letter to Leonard Clark, 3 February 1966 (Berg).

50. Hart-Davis, *Edmund Blunden*, n.p.

51. Letter to Leonard Clark, 18 December 1967 (Berg).

52. J. E. Morpurgo, "Edmund Blunden: Poet of Community," *Contemporary Review* 22, no. 1305 (1974):195.

53. Brander, "Edmund Blunden," p. 49.

54. "On Tearing Up a Cynical Poem," *A Hong Kong House*, p. 101.

55. Preface to *Poems 1930—1940* (London, 1940), p. vii.

56. "The Home of Poetry," *Shells by a Stream* (London, 1944), p. 1.

57. Charles Williams, "Edmund Blunden," in *Poetry at Present* (Oxford: Clarendon Press, 1930), p. 208.

58. "Change and Song," *Poems of Many Years* (London, 1957), p. 279.

Chapter Two

1. *Cricket Country* (London, 1944), p. 64.

2. Untitled memoir of his father (HRC).

3. Jon Silkin, *Out of Battle: The Poetry of the Great War* (London, 1972), p. 104.

4. Pocket-book, various notes on signalling & c., manuscript diary for opening of battle of Passchendaele (HRC).

5. *Nature in English Literature* (London, 1929), pp. 139—40.

6. *Keats's Publisher*, pp. 108—9.

7. "John Clare," *Sons of Light: A Series of Lectures on English Writers* (Tokyo, 1949), p. 35.

8. *Nature in English Literature*, pp. 11, 13, 32.

9. "Tradition in Poetry," *Tradition and Experiment in Present-Day Literature: Addresses Delivered at the City Literary Institute* (New York: Oxford University Press, 1929), p. 64.

10. *Nature in English Literature*, pp. 70—71.

11. J. C. Squire, "Mr. Edmund Blunden," in *Essays on Poetry* (London, 1923), p. 174.

12. "Chances of Remembrance," *Poems 1914—30* (London, 1930), p. 289.

13. "The Eclogue," *English Poems*, p. 68.

14. "The Fair Humanities of Old Religion," *Pastorals*, p. 32.

15. "Wild Cherry Tree," *Poems 1914—30*, p. 48.

16. "Again, What Is Poetry?" *The Mind's Eye*, pp. 227—28.

17. "Robert Bridges," *Sons of Light*, p. 135.

18. Letter to Edward Marsh, 21 November 1925 (Berg).

19. "The Pike," *The Waggoner and Other Poems* (London, 1920), p. 20.

20. "The Poor Man's Pig," *The Shepherd and Other Poems of Peace and War* (New York, 1922), p. 43.

21. "Tradition in Poetry," p. 66.

22. See, for example, "The Toad," *Choice or Chance* (London, 1934), p. 14.

23. Interview with John Press, printed in *The Poet Speaks: Interviews with Contemporary Poets*, ed. Peter Orr (London, 1966), p. 35.

24. *The Face of England*, p. 25.

25. See the section "English Studies: A Paradox," in *A Wanderer in Japan* (Tokyo, 1950), p. 13.

26. *Shelley: A Life Story* (New York, 1947), p. 226.

27. "Buxted," *After the Bombing* (London, 1949), p. 27.

28. "Triumph of Autumn," *Shells by a Stream*, pp. 9–10.

29. "Winter Ending," *Elegy*, p. 75.

30. "Into the Distance," *Choice or Chance*, p. 7.

31. "The Poor Man's Pig," *The Shepherd*, p. 44.

32. *The Face of England*, p. 55.

33. J.C. Squire, Letter to Edmund Blunden, 19 August 1930 (HRC).

34. *On the Poems of Henry Vaughan* (London, 1927), p. 45.

35. "Tradition in Poetry," p. 59.

36. Lectures on "Composition, inspiration and a few words on revision," autograph manuscript, undated (HRC).

37. Letter to Leonard Clark, 12 January 1964 (Berg).

38. Orr, *The Poet Speaks*, p. 35.

39. Both MS drafts of "The Poor Man's Pig" are contained in the "MS/Blunden/Works/9" folder of the HRC collection.

40. "The Unchangeable," *The Waggoner*, p. 22.

41. "Perch-Fishing," *The Waggoner*, pp. 43–45.

42. Robert Graves, "Dead Movements," in *The Common Asphodel: Collected Essays on Poetry, 1922–1949* (1949; reprint ed., New York: Haskell House, 1970), pp. 112–13.

43. Vivian de Sola Pinto, *Crisis in English Poetry: 1880–1940* (London: Hutchinson's University Library, 1951), p. 134.

44. "Lascelles Abercrombie," *Shells by a Stream*, p. 24.

45. "The Georgians," autograph manuscript, undated (HRC).

46. Harold Monro, "The Nightingale Near the House," in *The Collected Poems of Harold Monro*, ed. Alicia Monro (London: Cobden-Sanderson, 1933).

47. W. H. Davies, "All in June," in *Georgian Poetry*, ed. James Reeves (London: Penguin, 1962), p. 46.

48. Edmund Gosse, Letter to Edmund Blunden, 5 February 1923 (HRC).

49. "Poetical Reminiscences," autograph manuscript/notes, on Merton College stationery (HRC).

50. Robert Bridges, "On the Dialectal Words in Edmund Blunden's Poems," in *Society for Pure English Tract No. V* (Oxford, 1921), p. 26.

51. Even after their divorce, Mary Blunden could still supply Edmund with native knowledge of country words, or other information she had an alert ear for: ". . . . I heard a woman the other day call an earwig a twitchbell she says thats the name for them in Sunderland" (letter in the HRC collection, no date).

52. "In a Park at Kyoto," "The Inn Window, Fukuoka," and "A House in Ushigome," grouped as "Moments," in *Eastward* (Kyoto, 1949), p. 33.

53. "Far East," *Near and Far: New Poems* (London, 1929), pp. 22–23.

54. Robert Graves and Alan Hodge, *The Long Week-End: A Social History of Great Britain, 1918–1939* (New York: Norton, 1963), p. 217.

55. Antonio Amato, "Introduzione alle poesie di guerra di Edmund Blunden," *Le lingue straniere* 12, no. 3 (1963):16 (author's translation).

56. *Nature in English Literature*, pp. 100, 93, 102.
57. "The Hill," *Choice or Chance*, p. 4.
58. Preface to *The Face of England*, p. x.
59. *Nature in English Literature*, p. 149.
60. *Shelley*, p. 77.
61. "A Budding Morrow," *English Poems*, p. 55.
62. "Familiarity," *Near and Far*, p. 37.
63. Diary, 18 November 1939 (HRC).
64. Ivor Gurney, Letter to Edmund Blunden, undated (HRC).
65. "Evening Mystery," *The Shepherd*, p. 30.
66. "The Ambush," *Elegy*, p. 41.
67. "Winter: East Anglia," *English Poems*, p. 25.
68. "Water Moment," *English Poems*, p. 45.
69. "Brook in Drought," *English Poems*, p. 50.
70. "Man and Nature," *Addresses on General Subjects*, p. 62.
71. *Three Young Poets: Critical Sketches of Byron, Shelley and Keats* (Tokyo, 1959), p. 50.
72. Letter to John Masefield, 19 May 1966 (HRC).
73. Michael Thorpe, *The Poetry of Edmund Blunden* (Chatham, 1971), p. 24.
74. *The Face of England*, p. 144.
75. "Strange Perspective," *English Poems*, p. 85.
76. "Old Pleasures Deserted," *English Poems*, p. 88.
77. "To Nature," *English Poems*, p. 107.
78. "The Brook," *English Poems*, p. 102.
79. "A Song Against Hope," *Pastorals*, p. 13.
80. "The Kiss," *Halfway House*, p. 48.
81. "The Recovery," *Halfway House*, p. 69.
82. "The Country Tradition," *Votive Tablets* (New York, 1932), p. 262.
83. Silkin, *Out of Battle*, p. 120.
84. "Resentients," *English Poems*, p. 127.
85. "The Deeper Friendship," *Near and Far*, p. 55.
86. "Nature Displayed," *Retreat* (Garden City, N.Y., 1928), pp. 10, 9.
87. *The Bonadventure*, p. 170.

Chapter Three

1. "Misunderstandings," *English Poems*, p. 59.
2. "A Dream," *English Poems*, p. 83.
3. *The Face of England*, p. 19.
4. Diary, 28 January 1930 (HRC).
5. "Wild Creatures at Nightfall," *A Hong Kong House*, p. 72.
6. "The Preservation of England," *Votive Tablets*, p. 354.
7. "Gleaning," *The Shepherd*, p. 17.
8. "'Southern England' in 1944," *After the Bombing*, p. 35.
9. "The Crown Inn," *English Poems*, p. 28.
10. "Winter Nights," *Poems 1914–30*, p. 134.

11. "Herrick," *Votive Tablets*, p. 71.
12. *Cricket Country*, p. 98.
13. "Pride of the Village," *English Poems*, pp. 33, 31.
14. "Hammond (England)," *After the Bombing*, p. 45.
15. "The Season Reopens," *Poems of Many Years*, p. 283.
16. *Cricket Country*, p. 12.
17. Siegfried Sassoon, Letter to Edmund Blunden, 6 June 1939 (HRC).
18. Letter to Siegfried Sassoon, 8 June 1939 (HRC).
19. *Cricket Country*, p. 45.
20. Ibid., p. 141.
21. "'Line Upon Line,'" *The Mind's Eye*, p. 111.
22. Ibid., p. 112.
23. J. C. Squire, "Mr. Edmund Blunden," in *Essays on Poetry*, p. 178.
24. "A Family Discourse: Or, John Constable's Painting 'The Valley Farm,'" *A Hong Kong House*, p. 79.
25. See Blunden's remarks on the *genius loci* in the Preface to *The Face of England*, p. x.
26. "Country Characters," *Poems 1930–1940*, p. 191.
27. Renato Poggioli, *The Oaten Flute: Essays on Pastoral Poetry and the Pastoral Ideal* (Cambridge, Mass.: Harvard University Press, 1975), p. 5.
28. Postscript to Letter to Siegfried Sassoon, 13 November 1955 (HRC).
29. "Country Sale," *English Poems*, p. 20.
30. "Will o' the Wisp," *The Shepherd*, p. 32.
31. "A Yeoman," *English Poems*, p. 26.
32. "The Waggoner," *The Waggoner*, pp. 13–14.
33. "The Shepherd," *The Shepherd*, pp. 12–13.
34. "Mole Catcher," *The Shepherd*, pp. 34–55.
35. David Perkins, *A History of Modern Poetry: From the 1890s to the High Modernist Mode* (Cambridge, Mass., 1976), p. 222.
36. "Mole Catcher," *The Shepherd*, pp. 35, 34.
37. "Almswomen," *The Waggoner*, p. 15.
38. *The Face of England*, p. 51.
39. "A Poet's Death (1958)," *A Hong Kong House*, p. 96.
40. "Miss Warble," *The Mind's Eye*, p. 153.
41. *The Face of England*, p. 177.
42. John Masefield, Letter to Edmund Blunden, 30 June 1920 (HRC).
43. "Departed: or, 'tis Twenty Years Since," *Elegy*, p. 86.
44. "The Ornamental Water," *Shells by a Stream*, p. 15.
45. *The Face of England*, p. 4.
46. Diary, January 2, 1930 (HRC).
47. *The Face of England*, p. 63.
48. Ibid.
49. "Jim's Mistake," *Poems 1930–1940*, p. 242.
50. "Storm at Hoptime," *The Waggoner*, p. 49.
51. *Cricket Country*, p. 67.

52. Untitled memoir of his father, autograph manuscript, undated (HRC).

53. "Incident in Hyde Park, 1803," *Halfway House*, pp. 37—40.

54. Letter to Georgina Blunden, 30 September [1917?] (HRC).

55. *Charles Lamb and His Contemporaries* (Cambridge, 1933), p. 6.

56. *Nature in English Literature*, p. 99.

57. Introduction to *The Life of George Crabbe by His Son* (London: Cresset Press, 1947), p. xxiv.

58. *Nature in English Literature*, p. 154.

59. Henry Newbolt, *New Paths on Helicon* (London, 1927), p. 404.

60. *Shelley*, p. 276.

61. *Thomas Hardy*, pp. 163—64.

62. William Wordsworth, "Preface to *Lyrical Ballads*," in Criticism: The Major Texts, ed. Walter Jackson Bate (New York: Harcourt Brace Jovanovich, 1970), p. 336.

63. "Village," *English Poems*, p. 27.

64. "No Continuing City," *English Poems*, pp. 38—39.

65. Ancestral and personal notes, documents and memorabilia, autograph manuscript/notebook with loose notes, documents, etc. (HRC). Blunden's mother, one should remember, was also trained as a schoolteacher, and she taught with her husband in Framfield and, later on, Yalding.

66. *English Villages* (London, 1945), p. 8.

67. "The Complaint," *Retreat*, pp. 19—20.

68. See Chapter 5, "The Farmer's Boy," in *Nature in English Literature*.

69. Robert Graves, Letter to Edmund Blunden, undated (HRC).

70. Letter to Edward Marsh, 5 August 1924 (Berg).

71. *Nature in English Literature*, p. 156.

72. Preface to *Shelley*, p. xi.

73. "Victorians," *Poems 1930—1940*, pp. 252—53.

74. "Forefathers," *The Shepherd*, p. 14.

75. "April Byeway," *The Shepherd*, p. 82.

76. "The English Countryside," *The Mind's Eye*, pp. 157—58.

77. "Sixpence to the River," *Elegy*, p. 84.

78. "To Our Catchment Board," *Poems 1930—1940*, pp. 230—31.

79. "To Teise, A Stream in Kent," *Shells by a Stream*, p. 8.

80. "The Preservation of England," *Votive Tablets*, p. 356.

81. "Chaffinch: on Suburban Growths," *Elegy*, p. 87.

82. "On Preservation," *The Mind's Eye*, p. 178.

83. "The English Countryside," *The Mind's Eye*, p.154.

84. "Nature Displayed," *Retreat*, p. 9.

85. "Departure," *Retreat*, p. 52.

86. Letter to Claire Poynting Blunden, 18 April 1947 (HRC).

87. Robert Graves, "Modernist Poetry and Civilization," *The Common Asphodel*, p. 140.

88. "Man and Nature," *Addresses on General Subjects*, pp. 67—68.

89. *The Face of England*, p. 96.

90. "Ornithopolis," *Retreat*, p. 41.

91. "London: A December Memory," *Poems 1930–1940*, p. 195.

92. "On Preservation," *The Mind's Eye*, pp. 179–80.

93. "Minority Report," *Elegy*, p. 50.

94. Diary, 6 October 1939 (HRC).

95. *The Bonadventure*, p. 138.

96. Edmund Blunden, ed., *Return to Husbandry* (London: J. M. Dent and Sons, 1943).

97. "For the Country Life," *Shells by a Stream*, p. 11.

98. "The Survival," *Poems 1914–30*, p. 291.

99. Hugh I'Anson Fausset, "Edmund Blunden's Later Poetry," in *Poets and Pundits* (London, 1947), p. 195.

100. *The Face of England*, p. 108.

101. Ibid., p. 146.

102. "Yalding Bridges," *The Mind's Eye*, p. 170.

103. "On Preservation," *The Mind's Eye*, p. 177, 176.

104. "On a Journey, 1943," *Shells by a Stream*, p. 14.

105. *A Wanderer in Japan*, p. 6.

106. "To a Planner," *After the Bombing*, p. 31.

107. *English Scientists as Men of Letters: Jubilee Congress Lecture delivered on September eleventh, 1961 in Loke Yew Hall, University of Hong Kong* (Hong Kong: Hong Kong University Press, 1961), p. 3.

108. Letter to Edward J. Finneron, 20 December 1954 (HRC).

109. "Modern Times," *Eleven Poems* (Cambridge, 1965), p. 17.

110. Bernard Bergonzi, *Heroes' Twilight: A Study of the Literature of the Great War* (New York, 1966), p. 70.

Chapter Four

1. Preface to *Poems 1914–30*, p. v.

2. Letter to G. H. Grubb, 11 May 1930 (Berg).

3. The Somme Still Flows," *The Mind's Eye*, p. 43.

4. "Third Ypres," *Undertones of War*, p. 233.

5. Robert Graves, *Good-bye to All That* (Garden City, N.Y., 1957), p. 232.

6. "The Guard's Mistake," *Undertones of War*, p. 214.

7. "Vlamertinghe: Passing the Château, July 1917," *Undertones of War*, p. 229.

8. "La Quinque Rue," *Undertones of War*, p. 241.

9. "In Wiltshire," *Poems 1914–30*, p. 290.

10. "Preliminary" to *Undertones of War*, p. 11.

11. "A Sunrise in March," *Near and Far*, p. 46.

12. *The Faerie Queene*, VI.ix.29. Useful discussions of this idea in *The Faerie Queene* appear in Chapter 7 of Laurence Lerner's *The Uses of Nostalgia: Studies in Pastoral Poetry* (London: Chatto and Windus, 1972), and Peter V. Marinelli's

Pastoral (London: Methuen, 1971). My own awareness of the revitalizing "respite" was sparked by a stimulating lecture given by Professor Walter Kaiser of Harvard.

13. "Come On, My Lucky Lads," *Undertones of War*, p. 219.
14. "Preparations for Victory," *Undertones of War*, p. 218.
15. Letter to Charles Edmund Blunden, 26 June 1916 (HRC).
16. In *The Savage God* (New York: Random House, 1972), A. Alvarez describes Owen's task as a new one for a poet and warrior: a "double duty—to forge a language which will somehow absolve or validate absurd death, and to accept the existential risks involved in doing so . . ." (p. 245).
17. *The Great Church of the Holy Trinity, Long Melford* (Ipswich: W.S. Cowell, 1966), p. 13.
18. *Undertones of War*, p. 133.
19. Letters to Charles Edmund Blunden, 13 July 1916 and 28 May 1917 (HRC).
20. *Cricket Country*, p. 94.
21. "Bleue Maison," *Poems of Many Years*, p. 23.
22. "Gouzeaucourt: The Deceitful Calm," *Undertones of War*, p. 236.
23. "In May 1916: Near Richebourg St. Vaast," *Poems 1930—1940*, p. 201.
24. "At Senlis Once," *Undertones of War*, p. 220.
25. "The Camp in the Wood," *Poems 1930—1940*, pp. 205—6.
26. "The Zonnebeke Road," *Undertones of War*, p. 221.
27. "On Reading that the Rebuilding of Ypres Approached Completion," *Undertones of War*, p. 248.
28. "The Trees on the Calais Road," *Poems of Many Years*, pp. 22—23; "The Ancre at Hamel: Afterwards," *Undertones of War*, p. 242.
29. *We'll Shift Our Ground* (London, 1933), p. 39.
30. "A House in Festubert," *Undertones of War*, p. 213.
31. *Thomas Hardy*, pp. 239—40; Diary, 14 October 1939 (HRC).
32. "Rhymes on Béthune, 1916," *Poems 1930—1940*, pp. 203—4.
33. "Into the Salient," *Poems 1914—30*, p. 145.
34. "Rhymes on Béthune, 1916," *Poems 1930—1940*, p. 202.
35. "Premature Rejoicing," *Poems 1914—1930*, p. 142.
36. Frank Swinnerton, *The Georgian Literary Scene, 1910—1935* (London, 1950), pp. 268—69.
37. D. J. Enright, "The Literature of the First World War," in *The Modern Age*, vol. 7 of *The Pelican Guide to English Literature*, ed. Boris Ford (Baltimore: Penguin, 1964), p. 154.
38. *War Poets: 1914—1918* (London, 1958), p. 12.
39. Ibid., pp. 12—13.
40. *On the Poems of Henry Vaughan*, p. 34.
41. "The Soldier Poets of 1914—1918," introduction to *An Anthology of War Poems*, ed. Frederick Brereton (London: Collins, 1930), p. 24.
42. "An Infantryman," *Retreat*, pp. 26, 25.

43. "The Soldier-Poets of 1914–1918," p. 20.

44. Letter to Siegfried Sassoon, 3 May 1919 (HRC).

45. "Third Ypres," *Undertones of War*, p. 231.

46. "The Zonnebeke Road," *Undertones of War*, p. 221.

47. "Concert Party: Busseboom," *Undertones of War*, p. 224.

48. "The Prophet," *Undertones of War*, pp. 237–38.

49. "Third Ypres," *Undertones of War*, p. 232.

50. John H. Johnston, *English Poetry of the First World War: A Study in the Evolution of Lyric and Narrative Form* (Princeton, 1964), p. 247.

51. *Undertones of War*, p. 209.

52. Silkin, *Out of Battle*, p. 102.

53. "The Aftermath," *English Poems*, p. 105.

54. *Cricket Country*, p. 38.

55. Unidentified personal reminiscence, autograph manuscript, undated (HRC).

56. A. S. Collins *English Literature of the Twentieth Century* (London: University Tutorial Press, 1951), p. 54.

57. "In My Time," *Elegy*, p. 46.

58. "Fancy and Memory," *Halfway House*, p. 61.

59. "Recurrence," *Elegy*, p. 68.

60. "The Lost Battalion," *Choice or Chance*, p. 29.

61. "1916 seen from 1921," *Poems 1914–30*, p. 163.

62. "The Watchers," *Undertones of War*, p. 255.

63. "Their Very Memory," *Undertones of War*, p. 245.

64. "Illusions," *Undertones of War*, p. 216.

65. "Clear Weather," *Poems 1914–30*, pp. 41–42; "Picardy Sunday," *A Hong Kong House*, p. 66; "Over the Valley," *A Hong Kong House*, pp. 67–68.

66. "Flanders Now," *Undertones*, p. 254.

67. Letter to Siegfried Sassoon, 24 August 1926 (HRC).

68. Graves, *Good-bye to All That*, p. 107.

69. *Undertones of War*, p. 145.

70. "The Veteran," *The Waggoner*, p. 60.

71. G. H. Harrison, Letter to Edmund Blunden, 26 October 1952 (HRC).

72. "Fall In, Ghosts," in *Edmund Blunden: A Selection of his Poetry and Prose*, ed. Kenneth Hopkins (New York: Horizon Press, 1961), p. 251.

73. "II. Peter, ii. 22: 1921," *Undertones of War*, p. 239.

74. "Some Talk of Peace—," *Choice or Chance*, p. 28.

75. Diary, 4 January 1930 (HRC).

76. "Preliminary" to *Undertones of War*, p. 11. In 1930, Blunden's brother Gilbert published, at Hawstead, *De Bello Germanico: A Fragment of Trench History*, written by Edmund Blunden in 1918. This is the work Blunden is referring to. His description of it, although overly modest, is basically correct. The prose lacks the distinctive calm of that in *Undertones of War*.

77. Letter to G. H. Grubb, 11 May 1930 (Berg).

78. H. M. Tomlinson, "A Footnote to the War Books," *Out of Soundings* (London: Heinemann, 1931), p. 236.

79. *Undertones of War*, p. 64.

80. Ibid., p. 129.

81. "The Extra Turn," *The Mind's Eye*, p. 54.

82. See "Preliminary" to *Undertones of War*, pp. 11−12.

83. Ibid., p. 155.

84. "Values," *Near and Far*, p. 67.

85. *Undertones of War*, p. 59.

86. Ibid., p. 209.

87. Letter to Siegfried Sassoon, 15 July 1929 (HRC).

88. Letter to Siegfried Sassoon, 11 November 1929 (HRC).

89. Graves, *Good-bye to All That*, p. 91.

90. "English War-Literature: Mr. Churchill's Book Not Its Sole Support," autograph manuscript, undated (HRC).

91. J. Middleton Murry, Postcard to Edmund Blunden, undated (HRC).

92. Johnston, *English Poetry of the First World War*, p. 19.

93. Orr, *The Poet Speaks*, p. 37.

94. Johnston, *English Poetry of the First World War*, p. 303.

95. Maurice Bowra, *Poetry and the First World War* (Oxford: Clarendon Press, 1961), p. 35.

96. Siegfried Sassoon, Letter to Edmund Blunden, 22 August 1964 (HRC).

97. Letter to Siegfried Sassoon, 29 February 1964 (HRC).

98. Letter to ?, 23 January 1917. This letter appears as part of a group of letters home from the front later transcribed by Blunden, without the names of the recipients, in a separate manuscript (HRC).

99. Siegfried Sassoon, *The Memoirs of George Sherston* (Harrisburg, Pa.: Stackpole Books, 1967), p. 362.

100. "To W. O. and His Kind," *Poems 1930−1940*, p. 215.

101. R. M. S., review of *The Shepherd*, by Edmund Blunden, *New Witness*, 16 June 1922. Clipping annotated by Edmund Blunden (HRC).

102. Introduction to *The War: 1914−1918: A Booklist*, comp. Edmund Blunden, Cyril Falls, H. M. Tomlinson, and R. Wright (London: National Home Reading Union, 1929), p. 2.

103. *Charles Lamb and His Contemporaries*, p. 2.

104. E. M. Forster, Letter to Edmund Blunden, 1 May 1937 (HRC).

105. Siegfried Sassoon, Letter to Edmund Blunden, 26 May 1940 (HRC).

106. "An International Football Match," *Elegy*, p. 49; "A Window in Germany," "About these Germans," "In the Margin," "Exorcized," *Poems 1930−1940*, pp. 191−92, 225−27, 214−15, 216−17.

107. Preface to *Poems 1930−1940*, p. viii.

108. Diary, 6 September 1939 (HRC).

109. Diary, 6 October 1939.

110. Diary, 10 October 1939 (HRC).

111. Diary, 11 October 1939 (HRC).

112. "By the Belgian Frontier," *Poems 1930–1940*, p. 221.

113. Edmund Blunden, Introduction to *Poems of this War by Younger Poets*, ed. Patricia Ledward and Colin Strang (Cambridge: Cambridge University Press, 1942), p. xii.

114. "A Patrol," "The Boy on Leave," *Shells by a Stream*, pp. 4–6, 42–43.

115. "Nature and the Lost," *Shells by a Stream*, p. 40.

116. "A Prospect of Swans," "Dovedale on a Spring Day," *Shells by a Stream*, pp. 12, 18–21.

117. "The Halted Battalion," *After the Bombing*, p. 22.

118. "H-Bomb," *Poems of Many Years*, pp. 288–89; "A Sonnet after Listening to B. B. C. News, 12 November 1963," *Eleven Poems*, p. 16.

119. Siegfried Sassoon, Letter to Edmund Blunden, 18 February 1955 (HRC).

120. "At the Great Wall of China," *Poems of Many Years*, p. 295. While teaching at the University of Hong Kong, Blunden visited the People's Republic of China. He wrote Edward J. Finneron on 2 February 1956: "We found plenty of ordinary interest in China, and were not worried over View & c., but of course the political journalists here were ready to revile us on our return,—it is a melancholy thought that nothing of a simple humanity is spared, let alone supported, by these dreary factions" (HRC).

121. Letter to G. H. Harrison, 14 November 1961 (HRC).

122. Letter to Paul Engle, 10 December 1963. (Courtesy of Paul Engle.)

Chapter Five

1. J. C. Squire, "Mr. Edmund Blunden," p. 176.

2. Preface to *Poems 1914–30*, p. vii.

3. "Henry Vaughan," *Sons of Light*, p. 39.

4. "The Poet's Universe," *Addresses on General Subjects*, p. 4.

5. "Imagination and Society," *Addresses on General Subjects*, p. 50.

6. T. Earle Welby, "Mr. Blunden," in *Second Impressions* (London: Methuen, 1933), p. 146.

7. Kenneth Allott quoted by Margaret Willy in "The Poetry of Edmund Blunden," *English* 11, no. 66 (1957):215. Willy's remarks on Blunden's use of military imagery, alluded to at the beginning of the second section of Chapter 5, appear on p. 216 of her article.

8. "William Blake," *Sons of Light*, pp. 91–92.

9. "The Subtle Calm," *Elegy*, p. 30.

10. "What Is Winter?" *Shells by a Stream*, p. 4.

11. "Sheet Lightning," *The Shepherd*, p. 31.

12. "The Last Ray," *English Poems*, p. 40; "Timber," *Shells by a Stream*, p. 8.

13. "'A Wedding or a Funeral,'" *Votive Tablets*, p. 83.

14. Osbert Sitwell, Letter to Edmund Blunden, 6 September 1919 (HRC).
15. "The Child's Grave," *The Shepherd*, p. 83.
16. "A 'First Impression' (Tokyo)," *English Poems*, pp. 114—15.
17. Thorpe, *Poetry of Edmund Blunden*, p. 46.
18. "The Winter Walk," *Shells by a Stream*, p. 57.
19. "Joy and Margaret," *After the Bombing*, pp. 20—21.
20. Thorpe, *Poetry of Edmund Blunden*, p. 47.
21. "Children Passing," *After the Bombing*, p. 21.
22. "But At Last," *A Hong Kong House*, p. 93.
23. "The Midnight Skaters," *English Poems*, pp. 28—29.
24. "Winter Stars," *Halfway House*, p. 47.
25. Richard Church, "Edmund Blunden: Agonist," in *Eight for Immortality* (London, 1941), p. 62.
26. "The Poet's Universe," *Addresses on General Subjects*, p. 10.
27. "A Survivor From One War Reflects during Another," *Eastward*, p. 13.
28. Church, "Edmund Blunden," pp. 60—61.
29. "Third Ypres," *Undertones of War*, p. 233.
30. *We'll Shift Our Ground*, p. 133.
31. Ibid., p. 235.
32. "Gleaning," *The Shepherd*, p. 19.
33. "The May Day Garland," *The Shepherd*, p. 26.
34. "On Some Crocuses," *Halfway House*, p. 78.
35. "Weserland, 1939," *Poems 1930—1940*, p. 185.
36. "The Shadow," *English Poems*, p. 69.
37. "A Fading Phantom," *English Poems*, p. 70.
38. "The Deeps," *English Poems*, p. 116.
39. "Achronos," *English Poems*, p. 79.
40. Letter to Edward Marsh, 5 August 1924 (Berg).
41. "I Just Noticed . . . ," *Poems 1930—1940*, p. 255.
42. "A Connoisseur," *Near and Far*, pp. 63—64.
43. "The Lost Leader," *The Mind's Eye*, p. 169.
44. Hardie, *Edmund Blunden*, p. 26.
45. "Once on a Hill," *A Hong Kong House*, p. 39.
46. "Voice of Spring," *A Hong Kong House*, p. 33.
47. Richard Church, Letter to Edmund Blunden, 10 November 1937 (HRC).
48. *Shelley*, p. 131.
49. "An Ancient Goddess: Two Pictures," *Poems 1914—30*, pp. 127—29.
50. "The Excellent Irony," *Halfway House*, p. 77.
51. "Impromptu—upon reading Dr. Julian Huxley on Progress," *Eastward*, p. 35.
52. "A Chronomachy: Or Let the Best Man Win," *Poems 1930—1940*, p. 234.

53. "The Lawn—A Fragment of Family History, at a House in Tokyo," *Eastward*, p. 26.

54. "An Aside," *Halfway House*, p. 57.

55. "The Covert," *The Shepherd*, p. 46.

56. "The Watermill," *The Shepherd*, p. 48.

57. "The Extra Turn," *The Mind's Eye*, p. 54.

58. "Battalion in Rest," *Undertones of War*, pp. 227–28.

59. "The Passer-by," *Retreat*, p. 24.

60. "The Nun at Court," *Poems 1914–30*, pp. 325–28; "Thomasine," *Shells by a Stream*, p. 55.

61. "Harbour Sketch: Written in Absence," *After the Bombing*, p. 39.

62. "Village Song," *Poems 1930–1940*, p. 248; "Lonely Love," *Elegy*, p. 82.

63. "To—," *English Poems*, p. 119.

64. "Lovelight," "Fulfilment," and "Among All These," *Shells by a Stream*, pp. 43–44, 45–46, 48–49.

65. "Lovelight," *Shells by a Stream*, p. 43.

66. *Cricket Country*, p. 188.

67. *Nature in English Literature*, p. 55.

68. "The South-west Wind," *The Shepherd*, p. 47; "November 1, 1931," *Halfway House*, p. 67.

69. "The Kind Star," *Poems 1930–1940*, p. 188.

70. "A Not Unusual Case," *Poems 1930–1940*, p. 256.

71. "A Thought of the Downs," *Choice or Chance*, p. 22.

72. "The Victor," *Shells by a Stream*, p. 43.

73. "Time Together," *Shells by a Stream*, p. 48.

74. Diary, 20 February 1940 (HRC).

75. Diary, 25 February 1940 (HRC).

76. "Millstream Memories," *A Hong Kong House*, p. 50.

77. "Catherine Sings," *A Hong Kong House*, p. 81.

78. "Henry Vaughan," *Sons of Light*, p. 51.

79. "To a Spirit," *Retreat*, p. 55.

80. "'There is a Country,'" *English Poems*, p. 101.

81. "The Secret," *Retreat*, p. 60.

82. Ibid.

83. "The Gods of the Earth Beneath," *The Waggoner*, pp. 62, 67.

84. *Nature in English Literature*, p. 61.

85. "To the Memory of Coleridge," *Shells by a Stream*, p. 23.

86. "Omen," *English Poems*, p. 86.

87. "Summer Rainstorm," *Near and Far*, p. 49.

88. "Tradition in Poetry," *Tradition and Experiment in Present-Day Literature*, p. 57.

89. "Bells on the Breeze," *The Mind's Eye*, p. 148.

90. "Hardham," *Pastorals*, p. 33. (This poem makes up part of "Stane Street" in *Poems 1914–30*.)

91. "Mole Catcher," *The Shepherd*, p. 35.
92. "Ask Old Japhet," *Elegy*, p. 89.
93. "A Shadow by the Barn," *Halfway House*, p. 51.
94. "A Church," *Shells by a Stream*, pp. 13–14. Sassoon's "The Old Huntsman" similarly imagines God as a man of the country.
95. Armistice; A March," *Eleven Poems*, p. 12.
96. "In Memoriam, A. R.-I.: Yokohama, November 1938," *Poems 1930–1940*, p. 254.
97. "The Puzzle," *English Poems*, p. 38.
98. "The Storm," *Retreat*, p. 57.
99. "Report on Experience," *Near and Far*, p. 58.
100. "A Psalm," *English Poems*, p. 108.
101. "Running Stream," *Poems of Many Years*, p. 280.
102. "The Deist" concerns the trial of Thomas Woolston in 1728–1729 for publishing his *Discourse on the Miracles of Our Saviour*, and "The Atheist" is a monologue by Lord Eldon, as he thinks over the verdict in *Shelley* v. *Westbrook* —which deprived Shelley of his children.
103. Thorpe, *Poetry of Edmund Blunden*, p. 11.
104. Hoxie Neale Fairchild, *Gods of a Changing Poetry*, vol. 5 of *Religious Trends in English Poetry* (New York, 1962), p. 364.
105. Ibid., p. 379.
106. *Thomas Hardy*, p. 165.
107. Ibid.
108. Ibid., pp. 255–56.
109. "The Poet's Universe," *Addresses on General Subjects*, p. 39.
110. "Imagination and Society," *Addresses on General Subjects*, p. 47.
111. "Death of Childhood Beliefs," *The Shepherd*, pp. 74–76.
112. "The Immolation," *Retreat*, p. 58.
113. "Stormy Night," *Choice or Chance*, p. 35.
114. "The Spire," *Elegy*, p. 55.
115. Lecture on "Composition, inspiration and a few words on revision," autograph manuscript, undated (HRC).
116. *Shelley*, pp. 54–55.
117. Letter to Siegfried Sassoon, 27 September 1957 (HRC).
118. *Keats's Publisher*, p. 86.
119. *Charles Lamb and His Contemporaries*, p.133.
120. "Christmas Eve 1959," *A Hong Kong House*, p. 58.
121. "The Correlaton," *Near and Far*, p. 51.
122. "Chimes at Midnight," *Poems of Many Years*, p. 296.
123. T. S. Eliot, "The Silurist," *Dial* 83, no. 3 (1927):263.
124. "Religion and the Romantics," *Addresses on General Subjects*, p. 88.
125. Appended to "Religion and the Romantics," *Addresses on General Subjects*, p. 113.
126. "From the Flying-Boat," *After the Bombing*, p. 19.
127. "Cathedrals," *A Hong Kong House*, p. 69.

128. "Resentients," *English Poems*, p. 127.
129. Letter to Edward Marsh, 15 March 1925 (Berg).
130. *Three Young Poets*, p. 25.
131. "Into the Distance," *Choice or Chance*, p. 7.
132. Review of *Poems of Mao Tse-Tung*, tr. Wong Man. Typed carbon-copy manuscript with autograph note (HRC).
133. See John G. Mills, "Some English Poets in Japan," *Japan Quarterly* 3 (1956):502.
134. *A Wanderer in Japan*, pp. 28−29.
135. Diary, 18 November 1939 (HRC).
136. "A Change," *Poems 1930−1940*, p. 257.
137. "The Sum of All," *Poems 1930−1940*, p. 257.
138. "A Life's Unity," *A Hong Kong House*, p. 47.
139. "W. S.: Last Plays," *A Hong Kong House*, p. 97.
140. "Summer Storm in Japanese Hills," *A Hong Kong House*, p. 21.
141. *Charles Lamb and His Contemporaries*, p. 1.
142. *Leigh Hunt*, p. 84.
143. "Experience and Record," *Addresses on General Subjects*, p. 315.
144. *The Poet Speaks*, p. 37.

Chapter Six

1. David Daiches, *Poetry and the Modern World: A Study of Poetry in England between 1900 and 1939* (Chicago, 1940), p. 64.
2. "Criticism: Sidney to Arnold," *Addresses on General Subjects*, p. 186.
3. John Taylor, Letter to John Clare, 14 August 1820, as quoted in *Keats's Publisher*, p. 112.
4. *Leigh Hunt's "Examiner" Examined* (London, 1928), p. 64.
5. *Christ's Hospital* (London, 1923), p. 167.
6. See *Leigh Hunt*, p. 32; *Thomas Hardy*, p. 7; *Shelley*, pp. 8−9.
7. "The Biography of Shelley," *Votive Tablets*, p. 225.
8. *Leigh Hunt*, p. 203.
9. *Leigh Hunt*, p. 253; "The Biography of Shelley," *Votive Tablets*, p. 229.
10. "Jonathan Swift," *Chaucer to "B. V."*, p. 116.
11. Edmund Blunden, Introduction to *Selected Poems of Tennyson* (London: Heinemann, 1960), pp. 1-24.
12. "Authors to Whom I Return," *Study of English*, November 1963, p. 15. (Special Edmund Blunden issue of a monthly magazine published by the Kenkyusha Publishing Co. of Tokyo.)
13. "English Poetry," *Addresses on General Subjects*, p. 294.
14. "The Country Tradition," *Votive Tablets*, p. 255.
15. *Leigh Hunt*, p. 278n.
16. "Sir Philip Sidney," *Sons of Light*, p. 15.
17. Sherard Vines, *Movements in Modern English Poetry and Prose* (Tokyo: Ohkayama, 1927), p. 60.

18. Ward, *Twentieth-Century English Literature*, p. 181.
19. Edmund Gosse, Letter to Edmund Blunden, 5 February 1923 (HRC).
20. Thorpe, *Poetry of Edmund Blunden*, p. 30.
21. Preface to *English Poems*, p. 7.
22. Church, "Edmund Blunden: Agonist," p. 56.
23. F. R. Leavis, *New Bearings in English Poetry: A Study of the Contemporary Situation* (London, 1942), p. 68.
24. Cyril Connolly, manuscript of review of Blunden's *A Hong Kong House*; reviewed with Roy Fuller's *Collected Poems* and Alan Ross's *African Negatives* (HRC).
25. Siegfried Sassoon, Letter to Edmund Blunden, 21 May 1928 (HRC).
26. *Charles Lamb and His Contemporaries*, p. 42.
27. W. Jackson Bate, *The Burden of the Past and the English Poet* (New York: Norton, 1972), p. 115.
28. Letter to Siegfried Sassoon, 12 December 1937 (HRC).
29. Letter to H. M. Tomlinson, 20 September 1953 (HRC).
30. "Siegfried Sassoon's Poetry," *The Mind's Eye*, p. 284.
31. "Poetical Reminiscences," autograph manuscript/notes, on Merton College stationery (HRC).
32. Diary, 8 November 1940 (HRC); Letter to Claire Poynting (Blunden), 22 December 1943 (HRC).
33. H.M. Tomlinson, Letter to Edmund Blunden, 9 December 1925 (HRC).
34. Ian Donnelly, *The Joyous Pilgrimage* (London: J.M. Dent & Sons, 1935), p. 208.
35. *Leigh Hunt*, p. 102.
36. J. C. Squire, Postscript to Letter to Edmund Blunden, 19 August 1930 (HRC).
37. J. C. Squire, Letter to Edmund Blunden, 22 December 1949 (HRC).
38. Letter to Siegfried Sassoon, 4 February 1952 (HRC).
39. Siegfried Sassoon, Letter to Leonard Clark, 8 March 1951 (Berg).
40. Richard Church, Letter to Edmund Blunden, 15 November 1964 (HRC).
41. Richard Church, Letter to Edmund Blunden, 3 November 1961 (HRC).
42. Author's Note to *Choice or Chance*, p.v.
43. See Chapter 22 of *Cricket Country*, "On a Trait of English Poetry," pp. 208–18.
44. Preface to *Poems of Many Years*, pp. 16–17.
45. Welby, p. 145.
46. Sir John Betjeman, Letter to Edmund Blunden, 23 December 1960 (HRC).
47. Tribute from Sir John Betjeman in *Edmund Blunden: Sixty-Five*, pp. 24, 27.
48. Fausset, *Poets and Pundits*, p. 196.

49. Diary, 7 February 1941, (HRC).

50. Stephen Spender, *Poetry Since 1939* (1946; rpt, New York: Haskell House, 1974), p. 20.

51. H. W. Garrod, Letter to Edmund Blunden, 2 May 1938 (HRC).

52. C. Day Lewis, Letter to Edmund Blunden, undated (HRC).

53. C. Day Lewis, "Lines for Edmund Blunden on his Fiftieth Birthday," included in the program for the dinner given in Blunden's honor at the Garrick Club on 1 November 1946. Blunden's copy, which was signed by Philip Tomlinson, Rupert Hart-Davis, William Plomer, Stanley Morrison, Walter De la Mare, and T. S. Eliot, among others, is in the HRC collection.

54. H. W. Garrod, Letters to Edmund Blunden, 12 August 1953 (HRC).

55. "Edmund Blunden, British Poet, Dies," *New York Times*, 21 January 1974, p. 42, col. 1.

56. Letter to Robert Lowell, 27 May 1966 (Houghton).

57. Robert Lowell, Letter to Edmund Blunden, 25 June 1966 (HRC).

58. I. A. Richards, Letter to Edmund Blunden, 8 February 1966 (HRC).

59. Walter De la Mare, Letter to Edmund Blunden, 6 October 1950 (HRC).

60. Hardie, *Edmund Blunden*, p. 34.

61. *The Face of England*, p. 108.

62. *Leigh Hunt*, p. 102.

63. "November 1, 1931," *Halfway House*, p. 67.

Selected Bibliography

PRIMARY SOURCES

1. Major Collections of Poetry

Selected Poems. Edited by Robyn Marsack. Manchester: Carcanet New Press, 1982. A discriminating new collection, sensibly arranged and intelligently introduced.

The Harbingers. Uckfield: G. A. Blunden, 1916.

Pastorals: A Book of Verses. London: Erskine Macdonald, 1916.

The Waggoner and Other Poems. London: Sidgwick and Jackson, 1920.

The Shepherd and Other Poems of Peace and War. New York: Knopf, 1922.

To Nature: New Poems. London: Beaumont Press, 1923.

English Poems. London: Cobden-Sanderson, 1925.

Masks of Time: A New Collection of Poems, Principally Meditative. London: Beaumont Press, 1925.

Retreat. Garden City, N.Y.: Doubleday, 1928.

Near and Far: New Poems. London: Cobden-Sanderson, 1929.

The Poems of Edmund Blunden, 1914–30. London: Cobden-Sanderson, 1930.

To Themis: Poems on Famous Trials, with Other Pieces. London: Beaumont Press, 1931.

Halfway House: A Miscellany of New Poems. London: Cobden-Sanderson, 1932.

Choice or Chance: New Poems. London: Cobden-Sanderson, 1934.

An Elegy and Other Poems. London: Cobden-Sanderson, 1937.

Poems 1930–1940. London: Macmillan, 1940.

Shells by a Stream: New Poems. London: Macmillan, 1944.

After the Bombing and other short Poems. London: Macmillan, 1949.

Eastward: A Selection of Verses Original and Translated. Sone Sakai Nishizakai and Oshima, Tokyo: 1949.

Poems of Many Years. London: Collins, 1957.

A Hong Kong House: Poems 1951–1961. London: Collins, 1962.

Eleven Poems. Cambridge: Golden Head Press, 1965.

2. Major Books of Prose

The Bonadventure: A Random Journal of an Atlantic Holiday. New York: Putnam, 1923.

Christ's Hospital: A Retrospect. London: Christophers, 1923.

On the Poems of Henry Vaughan: Characteristics and Intimations, With his principal Latin poems carefully translated into English verse. London: Cobden-Sanderson, 1927.

Leigh Hunt's "Examiner" Examined. London: Cobden-Sanderson, 1928.

Undertones of War. New York: Harcourt, 1965. (Originally published 1928.)

Nature in English Literature. London: Hogarth Press, 1929.

Leigh Hunt: A Biography. London: Cobden-Sanderson, 1930.

De Bello Germanico: A Fragment of Trench History. Hawstead: G. A. Blunden, 1930.

Votive Tablets: Studies Chiefly Appreciative of English Authors and Books. New York: Harper and Brothers, 1932.

The Face of England in a Series of Occasional Sketches. London: Longmans, Green, 1932.

Charles Lamb and His Contemporaries. Cambridge: Cambridge University Press, 1933.

We'll Shift Our Ground, or Two on a Tour, almost a Novel. London: Cobden-Sanderson, 1933. (With Sylva Norman.)

The Mind's Eye. London: Jonathan Cape, 1934.

Keats's Publisher: A Memoir of John Taylor (1781–1864). London: Jonathan Cape, 1936.

Thomas Hardy. London: Macmillan, 1951. (Originally published 1942.)

English Villages. London: Collins, 1945. (Originally published 1941. Part of the Britain in Pictures series.)

Cricket Country. London: Collins, 1944.

Shelley: A Life Story. New York: Viking, 1947.

Sons of Light: A Series of Lectures on English Writers. Tokyo: Hosei University Press, 1949.

Chaucer to "B. V.": With an additional paper on Herman Melville: A Selection of Lectures given chiefly at Tokyo University. Tokyo: Kenkyusha, 1950.

A Wanderer in Japan. Tokyo: Asahi-shimbun-sha, 1950.

John Keats. Longmans, Green, 1950.

Lectures in English Literature. Tokyo: Kodokwan, 1952.

War Poets: 1914–1918. London: Longmans, Green, 1964. (Originally published 1958.)

Three Young Poets: Critical Sketches of Byron, Shelley and Keats. Tokyo: Kenkyusha, 1959.

Addresses on General Subjects connected with English Literature Given at Tokyo University and elsewhere in 1948. Tokyo: Kenkyusha, 1962. (A sequel to a volume published in 1949.)

SECONDARY SOURCES

Amato, Antonio. "Introduzione alle poesie di guerra di Edmund Blunden." *Le lingue straniere* 12, no. 3 (1963): 13–18. Thoughtful account of Blunden's war poetry; not always exact in its discussion of Blunden's view of nature in war.

Bergonzi, Bernard. *Heroes' Twilight: A Study of the Literature of the Great War.*

New York: Coward-McCann, 1966. Limited usefulness where Blunden is concerned, but overall a more reasonable treatment of the war writers than Johnston provides.

"Professor Edmund Blunden." *Charles Lamb Bulletin*, n.s. 6 (1974), pp. 121−24. A reprint of the London *Times* obituary for Edmund Blunden. Useful, if very brief, biographical outline.

Bridges, Robert. "On the Dialectal Words in Edmund Blunden's Poems." *Society for Pure English Tract No. V*. Oxford: At the Clarendon Press, 1921, pp. 23−32. A lively reference work that can be used in conjunction with the glossary Blunden himself provides in *The Waggoner*.

Chau Wah Ching, Lo King Man, and Yung Kai Kin, eds. *Edmund Blunden: Sixty-Five*. Hong Kong: Hong Kong Cultural Enterprise Co., 1961. A remarkable volume of tributes from writers and friends and family. Gives a genuine sense of the personal affection and literary esteem Blunden inspired.

Church, Richard. *Eight for Immortality*. London: J. M. Dent, 1941. Contains a spirited advertisement of Blunden's work by a committed antimodernist.

Daiches, David. *Poetry and the Modern World: A Study of Poetry in England Between 1900 and 1939*. Chicago: University of Chicago Press, 1940. Attempts to compare Blunden's work to that of the major modernists.

Fairchild, Hoxie Neale. *Gods of a Changing Poetry*. Vol. 5 of *Religious Trends in English Poetry*. New York: Columbia University Press, 1962. Slickly written, but wrongheaded, examination of religious elements in Blunden's work.

Fausset, Hugh I'Anson. *Poets and Pundits*. London: Jonathan Cape, 1947. Typical of some studies which underappreciate ideas in Blunden's work even as they praise its skill and feeling.

Fussell, Paul. *The Great War and Modern Memory*. New York: Oxford University Press, 1975. Despite some overworking of its thesis about the war and the development of the modern ironic consciousness, this remarkable social and literary history of the war has been justly praised and honored.

Graves, Robert. *Good-bye to All That*. Garden City, N.Y.: Doubleday, Anchor, 1957. Graves's youthful autobiography provides some information about his association with Blunden, but is interesting mostly as a sharp tonal counterpoint to the gentle beauties of *Undertones of War*.

————. *In Broken Images: Selected Letters of Robert Graves, 1914−1946*. Edited, with a commentary, by Paul O'Prey. London: Hutchinson, 1982. Gives a picture of Blunden's friendship and quarrel with Graves; also, a detailed look at Blunden's and Sassoon's objections to *Good-bye to All That*.

Hardie, Alec M. *Edmund Blunden*. Writers and their Work, No. 93. London: Longmans, Green, 1958. Gracefully written appraisal of Blunden's career and work by one who taught with him and knew him well.

Hirai, Masao, and Milward, Peter, S.J., eds. *Edmund Blunden: A Tribute* *from Japan.* Tokyo: Kenkyusha, 1974. An excellent collection of reminiscences of Blunden and brief studies of all aspects of his work.

Johnston, John H. *English Poetry of the First World War: A Study in the Evolution of Lyric and Narrative Form.* Princeton: Princeton University Press, 1964. Provocative, but ultimately unfair, devaluation of much World War I poetry for its failure to move from the lyric to the epic.

Kirkpatrick, B. J. *A Bibliography of Edmund Blunden.* Oxford: Clarendon Press, 1979. This enormous and meticulous work (725 pp.) instantly gives one an appreciation of Blunden's staggeringly large output of poetry and prose. Indispensable to further study of Blunden.

Leavis, F. R. *New Bearings in English Poetry: A Study of the Contemporary Situation.* London: Chatto and Windus, 1942. Appreciative of Blunden's work compared to the Georgians', this study has serious reservations about poetry Blunden published after his first successful volumes.

Newbolt, Henry. *New Paths on Helicon.* London: Thomas Nelson, 1927. Offers high praise for the authenticity of Blunden's nature poetry.

Orr, Peter, ed. *The Poet Speaks: Interviews with Contemporary Poets.* London: Routledge and Kegan Paul, 1966. Blunden discusses inspiration, his manner of composition, and the influence of painting on his work.

Perkins, David. *A History of Modern Poetry: From the 1890s to the High Modernist Mode.* Cambridge, Mass.: Belknap Press of Harvard University, 1976. Encyclopedic account of the first decades of modern poetry; includes a brief, useful treatment of Blunden's work.

Ross, Robert H. *The Georgian Revolt: Rise and Fall of a Poetic Ideal, 1910–1922.* London: Faber, 1967. Thorough account of the Georgian movement—of which Blunden was hardly a part. Useful background.

Sassoon, Siegfried. *Diaries: 1920–1922.* Edited and introduced by Rupert Hart-Davis. London: Faber, 1981. Touching account of Sassoon's early days of friendship with Blunden, "a living emblem of all that is finest in this hazardous world of dust and dreams."

———. *Siegfried's Journey, 1916–1920.* London: Faber, 1945. Part of Sassoon's unjustly neglected autobiography. Interesting for its account of his early literary career and the beginning of his lifelong friendship with Blunden.

Silkin, Jon. *Out of Battle: The Poetry of the Great War.* London: Oxford University Press, 1972. Thoughtful consideration of Blunden's perception of nature during war.

Squire, J. C. *Essays on Poetry.* London: Hodder and Stoughton, 1923. Interesting for its appreciation of the specificity of Blunden's nature poetry; deficient concerning Blunden as a poet of ideas.

Swinnerton, Frank. *The Georgian Literary Scene, 1910–1935: A Panorama.* London: Hutchinson, 1950. Contains a brief look, sentimental but appreciative, at Blunden's work.

Thorpe, Michael. *The Poetry of Edmund Blunden.* Chatham: W. and J.

Mackay, Bridge Books, 1971. A large part of this study treats Blunden's "Joy" elegies.

Today's Japan, March-April 1960. Reminiscences and affectionate appreciations of Blunden's work by those who were students, colleagues, and friends during Blunden's years in Japan in the 1920s and 1940s. Contains a useful bibliography.

Willy, Margaret. "The Poetry of Edmund Blunden." *English* 11, no. 66 (1957):213–17. Brief but useful highlighting of several aspects of the work.

Index